GUIDE FOR RECREATION LEADERS

Glenn Q. Bannerman
Robert E. Fakkema

John Knox Press
ATLANTA

DEDICATION

To all of our friends—bless you.

ACKNOWLEDGEMENTS

We are grateful to many people for making it possible for us to put together this recreation book. To all of you that have let us share our leadership with you—THANKS!

A special thank you goes to Sharon Fakkema and Evelyn Bannerman for typing the manuscript. Susan Marshall captured the spirit of recreation with her illustrations.

To our families we say thanks for your patience. Most of all, we thank you who have purchased this book. Please use it rather than letting it collect dust.

Library of Congress Cataloging in Publication Data

Bannerman, Glenn Q
   Guide for recreation leaders.

   Includes index.
   1. Recreation leadership. 2. Amusements. I. Fakkema, Robert E., 1920– joint author. II. Title.
GV14.5.B32 1975   790   74-28523
ISBN 0-8042-2154-5

10 9 8 7 6 5

Printed in the United States of America

Contents

Introduction 4

Part One

Chapter I. Value of Recreation/Play 5
Chapter II. Guidelines for Leaders 8
Chapter III. Planning 12

Part Two

Chapter IV. Party Starters 15
Chapter V. Group Stunts 20
Chapter VI. Mixers 26
Chapter VII. Games 37
Chapter VIII. Fun with Musical Movement 60
Chapter IX. Mental Teasers 73
Chapter X. Spoke Relays 84
Chapter XI. Outdoor Games 89
Chapter XII. Party Poke and Its Use 97
Chapter XIII. Fun with Informal Dramatics, Stories, and Puppets 104
Chapter XIV. Fun for the Handicapped 117
Chapter XV. Fun Songs 123
Index 128

Introduction

This book has been planned and written with the intent of helping recreation leaders help others in their recreation and play activities. People of all ages do play and engage in recreational activities during their leisure hours. Many organizations include recreation and play activities in their programs. Leaders are needed to plan and lead these activities, and it is our desire that this book provide assistance to these leaders.

The book is arranged in two sections. Part One includes a brief philosophy on recreation and play and some general and specific aids for the recreation leader. Part Two, the larger section, includes the instructions for a wide variety of activities listed under various recreational categories.

It is our suggestion that the recreation leader proceed by reading Part One as soon as convenient after receiving the book. Then, as recreational events are anticipated, begin to look for specific activities which will satisfy the purpose of the event, begin arranging these activities in a meaningful order, and think through how they will be presented.

A word to the new or hesitant leader of recreation: the only way to develop into an effective leader is to go ahead and lead whenever and wherever the opportunity provides. The would-be leader can even offer his services to groups and thereby gain needed experience. "Try it—you'll like it." The satisfaction which comes from helping others find enjoyment is tremendous!

We hope you will have fun helping others have fun!

✻

CHAPTER I

Value of
Recreation/Play

Recreation and play, no matter how the terms are defined, have apparently had a profound influence on man's nature and well-being through all the ages of the past. The primitive art found in the caves of prehistoric man, the sketches in the burial chambers of the Egyptian pyramids, the hieroglyphics of the Indians left on the rocks in the southwestern United States, the remains of the Mayan civilization on the Yucatan Peninsula, and the ruins of the Incas in the mountains of Peru indicate a propensity for play early in the life of man which has continued to our time.

And man plays today. All ages perform some kind of playful activity or engage in a recreational pursuit. Children are to be seen playing their traditional games on sidewalks, streets, and playgrounds. Young people dance, play musical instruments, rap on the street corner or in the local drug store, engage in athletics, and much more. Adults delight in travel, visiting friends, engaging in arts and other cultural activities, etc. And so it goes. Play is apparently inherent in the human makeup.

And evidence indicates a future in which recreation will remain important in the life of man. Leisure is becoming a larger and larger part of man's life, and the threat of boredom and idleness must be associated with it. Hopefully, man will be enabled to use his leisure wisely toward an abundant and full life. Recreation/play, if handled correctly, may be ways of contributing to a well-balanced life.

Recreation may be defined as engagement in those activities which give balance to life, provide for meaningful relationships with others, promote opportunities for creative experiences, and enhance self-understanding. *Play* may be defined as an attitude of freedom, exploration, and joy (celebration, if you will) found in everything man does, such as a child has in early years. Recreation and play are terms which will be used synonymously in this book and include elements of both definitions.

Recreation benefits the individual

1. Maintains a balance in life. The major portion of most of our lives is consumed by our vocations which do not always provide all the experiences for a well-rounded and satisfying life. The child who pursues an intellectual and academic discipline in school during most of his days may require free and creative experiences during his leisure hours to give balance to his life. Those who work at hard labor may need more intellectual pursuits and artistic outlets for balance. The office worker may require more physical acitvity. Recreation/play, when used wisely, provides for the abundant and well-balanced life.

2. Keeps fantasy and creativity alive. Leisure provides opportunity for daydreaming and problem-solving. Participants can explore their potentials in recreation as they interact with others and learn new skills. New insights about one's self emerge. New vistas for one's self-fulfillment are opened to the imagination.

3. Is good just for fun; there need really be no other purpose. The exhilaration and zest from the doing may be sufficient.

4. Maintains openness to new ideas and new friendships. The interaction with others through recreation and conversation opens the way to new meanings and new relationships.

5. Opens ways to possible vocations. New skills learned during recreation may be the first steps to a satisfying vocation in the future. The possibilities are endless. Skills in athletics may produce the professional athlete. Skills in art and drama may lead to future careers.

6. Opens ways to better understanding of self. Only as others respond to a person's words and behavior can that person understand what his nature and personality actually are. Recreation provides opportunities for these kinds of responses which, in turn, encourage the evaluation and redirection of one's own life.

7. Offers a blending of all of life. The attitude of play acquired in recreational activities may carry over into all of life, including work and worship, and provide a person with a sense of completeness and purpose.

Recreation benefits groups

1. Enhances group spirit. The involvement in common endeavors with friends and neighbors encourages contagious enthusiasm.

2. Helps an individual accept a meaningful role in the group. Through experimenting with his relationships in the group, a person discovers how he can best contribute to that group—whether it be as leader, follower, clown, or some other role—and helps provide oneness and completeness for the group.

3. Enhances group unity. The enjoyment with friends and the common acceptance of goals through play activities encourages a number of individuals to become a group.

4. Frees for other experiences. When a group has played, it is further enabled to work, worship, study, and engage in other efforts as a group.

5. Safety valve to maintain group integrity. Recreation may be employed to relieve friction between cliques and persons within the group. Ill feelings may be dissipated in a volleyball game or the ping-pong table.

Summary

The above is not intended to say that recreation is a cure-all for the problems of man, but it is one approach! It can be the means to the ends suggested above or it may be an end in itself—enjoying a beautiful cloud formation, the joy of friendships, the inner satisfaction of an activity worth doing and well done—merely for the joy of the doing. It gives meaning to a life which might otherwise be drab and directionless.

The best recreation is motivated by the inner needs of man and, in turn, satisfies those needs. Recreation motivated by outward stimuli, such as competition, drugs, and alcohol, is not the most satisfying of recreational outlets.

Recreation and play become a festival and celebration of life where a person is free to express his real self and is renewed by the experience.

CHAPTER II

Guidelines for Leaders

Role of the leader

The leader of a particular recreational event understands the purpose of the event (to get-acquainted, deepen the fellowship of the group, serve as introduction to or party for a workshop or conference, teach new square dances, or some other reason) and provides the activities and instructions for achieving the purpose.

He will have done his homework before the event to

—determine the nature and experience of the group.
—research possible activities.
—plan the order of activities.
—have alternatives ready in case some may be needed.

Qualities of the leader

1. He has confidence in his own ability, confidence which is derived from knowledge of materials and experience. His self-confidence stimulates the confidence of the participants.

2. He is tactful in responding to comments and actions of participants in a way that does not belittle or embarrass.

3. He can see the humor in unexpected situations and can respond with humor. He can laugh at his own mistakes and help others laugh at theirs.

4. He encourages the beginner through friendliness, demonstration of activities, or adequate instruction. There are times when the same activity may need to be explained in several different ways in order to be understood by different participants.

5. He is sensitive regarding his own leadership abilities, relies on his own experience, and is free to try different approaches and activities when needed.

6. He enjoys what he is doing and his enthusiasm is contagious.

Relationships of the leader

The leader has a variety of relationships to the group with which he is working.

1. Enabler—He provides and directs the activities appropriate for the occasion.

2. Example—He respects the dignity of others and expects the same from them.

3. Responder to needs—He is sensitive to the interests and moods of the group and his leadership changes accordingly. If a certain type of activity is going well, he may stay with it. If a group is not responding to a certain type of activity, he is free to try something different.

4. Participant—He participates in activities with the group where possible, injects his enthusiasm, and enjoys being one of the group. He participates fully, either as leader or one of the group.

Miscellaneous Helps

Following are some helpful ideas for the leader to have in mind in planning for and leading various types of groups:

1. Large Groups

There are some activities which work particularly well with large groups (big circle square dancing, musical mixers, certain games). However, a larger group may be divided into small groups in order to use activities usually more effective with smaller groups (chair games, circle games, some mental teasers, etc.)

Enthusiasm spreads rapidly in a large group when the proper activities are used (musical mixers, groups stunts, folk dancing). Consider formations carefully—there may be a great many people to keep organized. Large groups may be handled easily when seated or standing in an auditorium or in rows in the recreation hall (singing, group stunts, entertainment, etc.), large circle (or two or more circles inside each other) for dancing and mixers, a square for a series of games with lines competing, or with a number of small groups (relays, competitive games, circle games, etc.). The leader needs to consider carefully how to move with the least amount of confusion from one formation to another. For example, it is easy to move from a square to four circles (with each side of the square becoming a circle).

2. Small Groups

The leader may be able to get small groups active and organized more rapidly (party starters, group stunts, stunt songs). Participants can be moved more rapidly from one activity to another. The series of relays with two rows of chairs is an excellent way to get started or to use at other times during a recreation event for small groups.

3. Age Groups

The leader is often responsible for planning and leading recreation for specific age groups—children, youth, adults, older adults. Following are some factors to be considered:

a. Consider the background and experience of participants and plan accordingly. If the participants enjoy and have had experience with singing or story telling, the leader knows these activities can be used again (although perhaps in a more advanced or different way).

b. Avoid activities which conflict with economic or sociological backgrounds. For example, it may not be appropriate to use games involving articles of food with a poverty group or dancing in a community where dancing is not accepted. However, if a new activity is introduced, such as dancing, the leader should do the best he can to make it enjoyable.

c. Consider what participants will be doing immediately before and following the recreation event and provide for effective balance and transition. If they have been doing something active, they may respond best to activities of a quiet type. If a serious discussion or worship is to follow the recreation, there may need to be a transition from active to quiet activities before moving into the more serious portion of the program.

d. Lively activities which keep participants alert and moving generally prove effective for getting a group started.

e. Activities used with younger persons can usually be used with any older group providing the mood is right. For example, "Slap Jack" is an appropriate game for children in grades 1—2 but can be used with senior highs when the latter are in a carefree or childlike mood.

f. There are a few characteristics to be considered when planning for specific age groups:

Children generally have an abundance of energy which suggests lively and stimulating activities. The younger the child the more individual activity and less group activity. The younger the child the less coordination. The younger the child the less intellectual (avoid mental teasers more appropriate for older groups).

Youth usually respond well to mental stimulation (mental teasers) and competitive activities (sports, relays, competitive games).

Most *adults* need and respond well to social activities where there is much mixing of persons in the group.

When leading *families*, make an effort to keep all ages together and use activities which all can do. It may be helpful to place participants in a situation where older persons can assist the younger in the more difficult activities (children remaining with parents, etc.).

Summary

There are a number of considerations the leader should have in mind as he selects and directs activities for a particular recreational event:

1. Consider the background and experience of participants.

2. Consider possible alternatives for use with the group. Plan for more than it seems time will allow as activities may be completed more rapidly than expected.

3. Be prepared for the unexpected. If one type of activity does not gain a response, the leader should feel free to shift to something different.

4. Outline recreational event with appropriate activity categories intended to gain proper response and select effective activities under each category. For example, party starters (Droodles, Table Scavenger Hunt), mixers (Come Along, Arches, Squat), active games, etc.

5. Plan according to formations. Groups should be able to move from one formation to another with the least amount of effort (square of chairs to small circles to large circle, lines for relays, etc.).

6. Leader should be able to depend on own experience to determine what will gain a good response from various groups and be ready to change plans as the group situation changes.

7. Select activities under categories which do not contrast drastically with what participants have been doing immediately before the particular recreational event or will be doing immediately following the event. Closing a recreational period with stunts and then folk songs or spirituals before moving into a more serious presentation would be more appropriate than relay races.

CHAPTER III

Planning

Chapter One concerns the understanding of recreation/play theory. Chapter Two deals with knowing who we are as leaders in recreation. Now comes the time to put theory and leadership together into the planning of activities. Here is a good pattern to follow in planning:

A. WHO: Get to know as much about the prospective participants as possible—i.e. age, sex, socio-economic background, likes, dislikes, working schedules, etc.

B. WHY: Why is the program being planned? Does the group need encouragement in getting to know each other on an informal basis? Does the group need an event just for socializing, with no real purpose other than that?

C. WHAT: What type of event will carry out the purpose of why? An example: If a group needs to be given an opportunity to get to know each other better, a home pot-luck supper might be more beneficial than a roller skating party.

D. WHEN: Many an event has not been well-attended because of conflicting schedules. Find out when the majority of people can participate in any given event.

E. WHERE: Time spent getting to and from an event is important. Physical facilities must be checked out. If you depend on a record player for a square dance, will you have adequate electricity? How about lighting, floor surface, water, etc. *Know* where you will be meeting!

F. HOW: After checking out the 5 W's comes the "how to" of getting it done. Committees may be formed to implement the action. Remember—the more people involved in the preparation, the more interest in the event!

Many people have gone home with a "blah" feeling because the leaders didn't think through the flow of the events. Questions often asked are: How will events progress from one to another? How will chairs be moved from one formation to another? How will participants be moved into different size groups, i.e. twos, fours, sixes, eights? How can one quiet a group? How? How? The foregoing questions are but a few that should be answered as the program is planned. A simple rule to follow:

Chart it out with words and diagrams to check the proposed program—

Event	Formation	Equipment Needs
Choo Choo		Music
String Speedway		Chairs, loops of string
Store		Chairs
Poison Pass		Chairs, balloons, music
Alley Cat Dance		Music
Big Circle Square Dance		Music

Planning the event

What committees are needed? The following might be considered: program, publicity, decorating, refreshment, and clean-up. It is always helpful to have representatives of each committee on the program committee.

Responsibilities of the committees:

Program: The program committee should set the theme of the event if there is to be one. They should pass along needs to various committees and provide the necessary leadership for implementing the activities.

Publicity: Eye appeal is the key to publicity, which should be catchy, different, charming, unique, and easy to understand. Give all ideas a chance. A mimeographed postcard usually doesn't communicate much enthusiasm for an event.

Decoration: Decorations do not have to be elaborate to be attractive. Use lighting to help get the desired atmosphere. Be on the lookout for display decorations at department and grocery stores. Many times the management will be glad to give them away. After use, collect and save for next year. Develop a decoration storage to help keep down costs.

Refreshments: Taste and eye appeal are the keys. *Elaborate* doesn't necessarily mean *good.* Plan the refreshments so that the committee will be able to take part in the party activities.

Clean-up: Too often the mess from a party is left for someone else to clean up. Many hands make light work.

*
CHAPTER IV
Party Starters

The activities in this category are intended for use at the beginning of a party or other informal social activity (drop-ins, with a few invited guests, before business meetings, etc.). The first person who arrives should have something to do! However, they may be easily adapted for use at other times. The following are intended mainly for youth and adults but may be adapted to the interests of younger groups or children with their families. And there are other games and activities which can be adapted for this purpose.

Smellavision. Prepare in advance 10—12 pill bottles containing cotton and a small amount of fluid with a distinguishing odor—perfume, shaving lotion, vinegar, ammonia, etc. Use fluids which cannot be identified by their color. Number each bottle. Scatter the bottles on two or three tables to allow access for a number of early arrivals. Give each guest a card and pencil and ask him to identify the odors. If desired, two or more guests may work together. When it is time to begin the next activity the answers may be given even though some participants have not yet finished. This may be done verbally or the answers posted on a wall or written on a blackboard.

Feelavision. Similar to the above. A number of socks are stuffed with various objects—ping-pong ball, can opener, ring, bracelet, etc. Number the socks and hang them on a cord, place them on a row of chairs, or distribute them on tables. As each guest arrives, give him a card and pencil and ask him to identify the contents.

What's in the Bag? Similar to "Feelavision." Using large paper bags, place objects in them which can be found with little difficulty in the kitchen of any home—beans, rice, raisins, soap, pepper can, spatula, pot holder, silverware, slices of bread, and so on. Participants may feel and shake the bags in order to determine the contents. Number the bags and ask the guests to write their guesses on a sheet of paper which is provided them as they arrive.

Newspaper Golf. Tape sheets of newspaper "greens" to the floor around the playing area (or begin in one room, go down a hallway, into another room, etc.). Place books, chairs, magazines, etc., on the floor between the greens to serve as obstacles. Holes are crayoned circles in the center of the greens and are numbered. Clubs are yardsticks, laths, or tree limbs about three feet in length which must be held close to the top when in use. Balls are checkers or small blocks of wood. Furnish score cards as guests arrive and let them begin playing immediately. A player may start at any green.

Guess Who. As the guests arrive for the party, place the name of some well-known personality on the back of each person. The guests do not know whose names they are. Each guest moves around the playing area asking questions about his name, questions which may only be answered by "yes" or "no." As soon as a guest learns his name, he may move on to another activity. Names may be used which apply to the occasion or party theme, such as different toys for a Christmas party, funny paper characters for a Comic Caper, or important government people for a "political" party.

Egg Blowing. Carefully empty eggs ahead of time by puncturing both ends with a pin and blowing out the contents (do this when having scrambled eggs for breakfast!). Use a card table with one or two persons kneeling or sitting on each side with chins on the edge of the table. The object of the game is to attempt to blow the egg across the opposite edge of the table and, at the same time, preventing opponents from doing the same on your side. A ping-pong ball may be used if breakage is too rapid.

Matching Beans (Odd or Even). Give each person the same number of beans (15—20 is a good number). On a signal to begin, each guest may hold as many of his beans in one of his hands as he desires, approach another guest, extend the hand containing the beans, and ask, "Odd or even?" If the person holding the beans should have an odd number of beans in his hand and the guesser says "Odd," the beans are given to the one guessing. Otherwise, if the guesser says, "Even," he must give up an equal number of his beans. Peanuts, beads, or a number of small objects may be used in place of beans to suit the theme of the occasion.

Don't Say "Yes." Give each guest a supply of dried beans when he arrives (15 is a good number). During conversation with other guests, each participant tries to get them to answer "yes" to questions. If a guest says "yes," he must give one bean to the person who questioned him. Allow the game to continue for a short time and then ask for those with the most and the fewest beans in their hands. This may also be done by trying to avoid using the word "I".

String Handcuffs. Cut enough string in advance to supply each guest with one piece approximately four feet in length. Ask each guest to tie a loop on both ends of his piece of string, large enough to slip a hand through. Avoid slip knots if possible. Two guests work together. One guest slips his hands through the loops of his piece of string. The guest working with him slips one hand through one of the loops on his own string, places the other end of the string over and around the string of his partner, and places his second hand through the second loop of his string. The two players are now "handcuffed." The problem is to separate themselves from each other without breaking or untying the string or sliding a loop over one of the hands.

Solution: Give the following instructions to one of the two players: "Grasp the middle of your piece of string. Slip it through one of the wrist loops of your partner, moving from the elbow side toward the hand. A loop is formed as the string comes through. Do not let the loop become twisted. Widen the loop and slip it over the hand of your partner. Pull the two ends of your piece of string and it will fall free."

Droodles. Post droodles around the walls of the playing area. These may be sketched on sheets of typing paper or poster board. As the guests arrive they are given paper, or 3 x 5 cards, and pencil and asked to number the paper from 1 to 20 (depending on the number of droodles). Participants are then asked to identify the droodles and write on the paper after the appropriate number what they think the pictures represent. The fun is in the answers given by the guests as their imaginations go to work. The leader then tells what the "artist" had in mind. Twenty droodles are shown on the next page. (See also *Droodles* by Roger Price, published by Price-Stern, 1965.) The artist's conceptions are as follows:

1. A bird's eye view of a Mexican boy riding a bicycle.
2. A rich sardine in its private can.
3. A worm taking a date to dinner.
4. A people neck sweater for turtles.
5. A $15.00 hamburger.
6. A drunken road crew and a sober line maker.

DROODLES

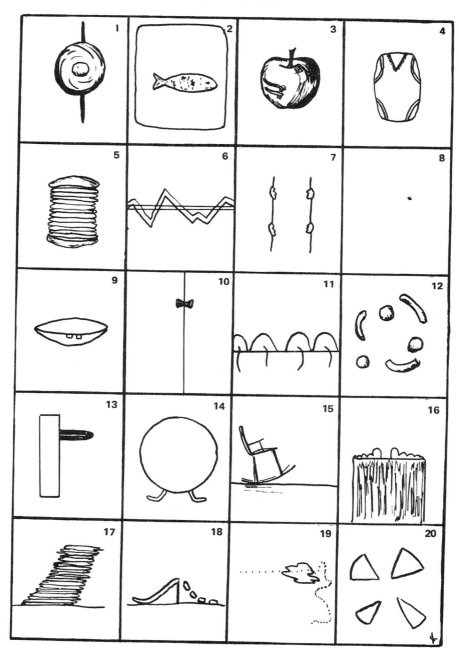

7. A bear climbing a tree.
8. A ghost with a cinder in its eye.
9. A clam with buck teeth.
10. A man with a bow tie caught in an elevator door.
11. The rear view of a rat race about to start.
12. A donut remnant sale.
13. A tall man in a phone booth playing a trombone.
14. A boy winning a bubble gum blowing contest.

   or

   A fat woman bending over.
15. "Whistler's Mother" out looking for Whistler's father (for artists)

   or

   A lunatic—someone off his rocker
16. A fish's eye view of a bathing beauty getting ready to take a dive.
17. Leaning tower of pizza.
18. A determined worm climbing over a razor blade.
19. A string of ants crawling through a puddle of champagne.
20. A four-way cold tablet going all four directions at once.

CHAPTER V

Group Stunts

The activities described under this category are intended for use in getting activities started and to restore interest when participation begins to lag. When several of these are used one after the other rather rapidly, groups are apt to become deeply involved. They may be led with any age group (and family groups) in almost any situation, although they are particularly effective with auditorium and banquet formations. They are excellent means for gaining group involvement and, although they may be used with any size group, they are particularly effective with large groups.

Crossed Wires. Ask participants to clap their hands together in front, raise their hands in the air, put their hands on their head (and other motions), and then grasp their nose with their right hand and their right ear with their left hand. The leader demonstrates as he gives instructions. Check to see whether everyone has the proper positions. If necessary, repeat instructions. Clap hands together again in front and return hands to nose and ear. Repeat this last portion once or twice and then give the instruction to reverse the holds (left hand on nose, right hand on left ear). Confusion reigns! Move quickly to another group stunt.

Variation: *Double Crossed Wires.* With two persons facing each other, ask each player to point to the other person's nose with the left hand, place right hand on the other's right ear, etc.

Clap-Pass. The leader raises his hands above his head and moves them from right to left and left to right so that they pass each other. Instruct the participants to clap their hands each time the leader's hands pass. They are to remain silent if hands do not pass. By working faster and faster, stopping suddenly, beginning to pass hands and then stopping suddenly, the leader can cause amusing confusion.

Clap Alphabet. Teach the group to recite the alphabet and spell words by means of a system of clapping. Each letter is prefaced by clapping a basic rhythm: 1–, 2–, 1, 2, 3 (a brief hold after the first two claps and then three rapid claps). "A" adds a miss (hands passing each other) after the basic clap: 1–, 2–, 1, 2, 3, miss. "B" is the basic clap, miss, clap. "C" is the basic clap, miss, clap, and miss. The remainder of the alphabet continues by adding and alternating misses and claps. Practice several letters and then spell a word—cab, bad, fad. Increase the speed as the group learns the rhythm. One group of junior highs learned this stunt after lunch at camp and it became a popular means for sending messages to each other.

Mirrors. Two participants face each other. They determine who will be number "1" and number "2". Ask those who are number "1" to be mirrors. Their partners perform motions—patting head, clapping hands, patting knees, pointing to the nose, etc., and number "1" must mirror the motions. After a few minutes of this, switch sides and repeat.

Counting Fingers. Two participants face each other. Each holds his closed fists in front of his chest. The leader counts "one, two, three." On the count of "three," each player holds up any number of fingers or keeps fists closed. The object is to see which player can first call out the total number of fingers held up on all four hands. Repeat several times and keep score.

House of Hands. Ask each participant to hold his hands in front of him with palms and fingers together and fingers pointed up. Place the knuckles of the middle fingers together. Explain that this is a house with the middle fingers representing the roof and the other fingers representing the people who live in the house. The little fingers are the children and, since they are small, they can be easily separated (the leader demonstrates as members of the group participate in the action). The thumbs are the grandparents, and they can be separated and placed in different rooms if they get into an argument. The index fingers represent the parents who live in the house, and they too can be separated (although this is more difficult for some than for others). But the ring fingers are the newlyweds, and you cannot separate them "without raising the roof!"

Variation: See "Scotchmen's Money" in Helen and Larry Eisenberg's *Omnibus of Fun.*

Shouting Names. This is a good stunt for a group where everyone is seated. On the signal to begin, everyone stands and shouts his first name. On a second signal, everyone sits and shouts his last name.

Repeat again for more volume. This can be used as an excuse to become better acquainted and to learn everyone's name!

Donkeys, Goats, and Monkeys. This stunt can be used immediately following the one above. Now that the names have been learned the mental capacities of the members of the group are to be tested. Three games are played to test the intellectual level of the participants. Everyone stands to begin the stunt. Anyone making a mistake must be seated and qualifies for that particular intellectual level. Those left standing at the end of the series can be considered human!

To test for "donkeys," play "Birds Fly." The leader raises his arms and shouts "Robins fly" (or some other bird or object). If what he says is a bird, everyone else raises his arms and shouts the same thing. If what he says is not a bird (house fly, tiger, rabbit, etc.), no one is to make a motion or say anything. Anyone doing so sits down.

To test for "goats," play "Do This, Do That." When the leader says "Do this" and follows it with a motion (clapping hands, putting one or two arms in the air, scratching head, etc.), everyone is to repeat the same motion. When he says "Do that" and follows it with a motion, no one is to repeat the motion. Those who do sit down and qualify as "goats."

To test for "monkeys," play "Open Shut." Teach the following rhyme to the group and ask them to repeat the rhyme while performing the appropriate motions:

Open, shut, open, shut, give a little clap,
(Fists held in front of each person and opened and shut with the corresponding words)
Open, shut, open, shut, put them in your lap.

Instructions are then given to recite the poem and to do what the leader says rather than what he does. He may say "put them on your shoulders" as he puts them on his head. The tendency will be to follow the motion. Move along with this game quickly. Otherwise, some participants will learn to close their eyes so they will not make a mistake. Those who make an error are seated.

Stand a Minute. On the signal to begin, everyone stands, places his hands behind his back (cannot have anyone looking at his watch!), stands for what he thinks is one minute, and then sits down. It is amazing how many will underestimate the length of a minute. Some will usually be seated after 15 seconds.

Shaking Hands. Use this stunt for a large group where it is seated n rows in an auditorium. Ask everyone to stand and stretch his hands over head. When the signal is given, they are to turn around and shake hands with the person behind them. Of course, there is no one with whom to shake hands because everyone has turned around! Instructions may also be given to shake hands to the right or to the left with the same result. This stunt usually gets a good laugh when the group realizes what has actually happened.

Heads or Tails. This stunt is used when the guest are seated. The group is divided into two sections. One section is designated as "heads," the other "tails." The leader flips a coin. If it lands "heads," those on the "heads" side of the group hold their right hands above their heads and keep them there. If the coin lands "heads" a second time, they raise their left hands; third time, right foot; fourth time, left foot, and the fifth time, they can put their hands and feet down. If the coin lands "tails," those on the "tails" side of the group follow the same procedure. The section to put its hands and feet down first is declared the winner. If it works out that both sections have their hands and feet in the air at the same time, this is the moment to tell a joke or short story!

Johnny Says: This is a good stunt to use when the members of the group are standing together and ready to move into a new formation. The leader makes a statement such as "Johnny says put your hands on your head" or "Clap your hands" as he performs the motion himself. If the leader includes "Johnny says" in the statement, the members of the group are to perform the same action. If he does not include "Johnny says" in his instructions, everyone should remain quiet. After a series of these statements the leader may say "Johnny says everyone move into a big circle with hands joined" or whatever formation he desires to use next. The group is now ready for the next activity.

Oomp–Bean–Soup. The leader divides the group into three sections and assigns a rhythm to each as follows:

First Section: "Oomp-bean-soup"
Second Section: "Clank-chizzle-chizzle"
Third Section: Sings
    "Oh where, oh where has my little dog gone,
    Oh where, oh where can he be
    With his tail cut short and his ears cut long;
    Oh where, oh where can he be?"

Direct the singing of the song to make certain everyone is familiar with it. Then direct each section separately as it practices its rhythm When the group is ready, the first group starts chanting its rhythm with a fast, steady tempo. After repeating it two or three times, the second section begins. Two or three more times and the third section starts singing in the same rhythm. Continue the stunt until the song has been sung twice by the third section. The object is to see who can make the most noise! Rotate the rhythms and repeat the stunt so that each section has an opportunity to try each rhythm.

Mathematics. This is an experiment to find out how well the members of the group can count. The leader asks the group to count with him and alternate numbers. The leader may say "1", the group "2", the leader "3", and so on. After the group has successfully counted several numbers in this series, start another series with a larger number. On the last series the leader should start with "4093" or some odd number close to it, so that the group will be counting on even numbers. When "4100" is reached, and if a fast counting tempo is maintained, the majority will call out "5000." Sometimes it takes a little explanation for members of the group to realize what they did wrong. Confusin' but amusin'! This does not work with junior age children (9−11). They have only recently learned to count this high and do not make the mistake!

Follow this with a stunt in which the group answers the mathematical questions of the leader. Encourage prompt answers. If the group starts off too slowly, the first question should be repeated in order to get a faster reaction. How much is 2 times 2? 4 times 4? (If someone says "8," start again.) 16 plus 10? 10 divided by 2? How many one-cent stamps in a dozen? How many two-cent stamps in a dozen? Of course, there are always 12 in a dozen! Many will say "6".

"Hare Today, Goon Tomorrow." The following story is told by the leader. As he performs the motions indicated in the parentheses, the members of the group do likewise. The humor is contained in the punch line at the end of the story.

"Once upon a time, there was a little rabbit (forefingers at side of head for ears) who lived in a little red barn (sketch shape of barn in air with hands). Every day he went out to the field and saw the mice running back and forth (index fingers waving back and forth past each other in front of the body) and he would grab two of them and crack their heads together (motion of grabbing one with each hand and hitting clenched fists together). The next day . . ." (Repeat the same story and action for three or four days. Then continue:) "One day his fairy godmother showed up (hold thumbs and index fingers of both hands together over head like a halo) and threatened to turn him into a goon (draw down corners of mouth with fingers) if he ever did it again." Continue the story with the rabbit, the barn, and the mice running back and forth, and the rabbit just standing and watching them. "Then one day the temptation was too much for him and he forgot what his fairy godmother had said and he grabbed a couple of mice (motion) and hit their heads together (motion). The fairy godmother (halo) appeared and turned him into a goon (motion). And the moral of this story is "Hare today (rabbit ears) and goon tomorrow (draw down corners of mouth)!"

Head and Shoulders. There are a number of excellent stunt and motion songs which can be introduced to accomplish the same purpose as these stunts. Only one is described here. Others are included in separate resource materials on songs.

Sing the following words to the tune of "Tavern in the Town" and accompany the singing with motions of placing both hands on the parts of the body indicated:

"Head and shoulders, knees and toes, knees and toes,
Head and shoulders, knees and toes, knees and toes,
Eyes and ears and mouth and nose,
Head and shoulders, knees and toes, knees and toes."
Repeat the stunt one or two times and increase the tempo.

CHAPTER VI

Mixers

The activities in this category are designed to promote group involvement to help participants feel more at ease with each other and, in some cases, to learn names and arrange guests into formations and groups for the activities which are to follow. If more than one mixer is used, the tempo should be rather rapid. This maintains involvement and prevents self-consciousness. It is suggested that these activities be used near the beginning of a social event although many are appropriate games for other times.

Musical Mixers

Come Along. No partners required. Participants stand in a circle with left hands extended toward the center. One player is asked to stand in the center of the circle. On the signal to begin, the player in the middle begins walking counterclockwise around the circle, takes the left hand of one of the other players with his right hand and continues walking, the second person grabs the left hand of another player with his right hand, and so on until a large part of the group is inside the circle moving around with the leader. At a given signal, each player rushes for his original position (including the first person who returns to his place in the edge of the circle). The last one in place starts the next game. If the group is large, two or more players should start in the center of the circle. A record player is one of the best methods for starting and stopping the game—play music while group is marching, stop it as a signal to return to original positions. Alarm clock, whistle, or some other means may be used. (20 or more participants, juniors through young adults.)

It is difficult to determine who were the last ones to return to their original positions if the group is large and there are a number of players in the center. This may be resolved by asking a specific number of players to start out as leaders when the music begins—

nyone who wants to but no one who has started as a leader before. If this activity is used in a party with juniors or junior high young people and the leader anticipates pairing them off into couples later, he mixer may be varied by asking girls to take the hands of boys and boys to take the hands of girls. Boys in this age group are sometimes eluctant to hold the hands of the girls! This variation will help prepare them for later activities.

Arches. This is an excellent activity for moving a group into couples. The participants are standing in a single circle. Two or more couples, depending on the size of the group, are selected to make arches like "London Bridges" at different points around the circle, gents on the inside facing out and holding the hands of the ladies on he outside. When the music begins (or some other signal), the other participants walk single file one direction around the circle and under he arches. When the music stops, the arches are brought down and hose caught in the arches, or the next players approaching the arches, are sent to the center of the circle to get partners. Ladies and gents pair off in the center and return to the circle to form additional arches. If too many of one sex are caught and sent to the center, some will have to wait for the next time the music stops to get a partner. The activity continues until everyone has a partner. The mixer develops momentum and excitement as it progresses. The group may now be directed in an activity which requires partners. (20 or more participants, juniors through young adults.)

Tunnel Chase. Circle of arches, as at completion of previous game, with gents on the inside facing and holding the hands of the ladies on the outside. An extra player starts through the arches and stops under one of them. The two persons making this arch run in *opposite* directions through the arches to see who can get back first. The first player returning becomes the partner of the player who began the mixer. The game continues with the new extra player moving. Be careful to avoid head-on collisions! (For small groups only, juniors through young adults.)

Squat. Double circle of couples with gents on the inside facing the ladies on the outside. When the music begins (or other signal), the inside circle (gents) move in one direction single file and the outside circle moves in the opposite direction. When the music stops, each player runs to find his partner, joins both hands, and squats. The last couple to squat may be dropped from the next march, or it may be better to leave them in and just give them a big "horse laugh." When the music starts again, everyone gets into the same circles and marches. Repeat several times. The mixer may be varied by asking participants to change partners when the music begins and promenade. The gents are then asked to reverse direction and everyone must find his new partner when the music stops. (20 or more participants, juniors through young adults.)

Variation: instead of squatting, ask partners to link elbows back to back and squat, or ask the gents to kneel on one knee and have the ladies on the other.

Island Mixer. This is an excellent mixer for the beginning of a recreation event. Have a number of different sized chalk circles drawn on the floor before the mixer begins (twine, newspapers, or different sized pieces of cardboard may be used.) Have enough "islands" so that there is room on them for all the participants to stand. As music is played, the guests walk anywhere in the playing area except on the islands. When the music stops, everyone tries to get on an island so that all his weight is supported inside the circle (some may be a little crowded—it is all right to have one foot in the air). Each time the music begins and the group starts walking again, erase one or more of the islands or make them smaller. This makes it more difficult for everyone to get on an island. This mixer is guaranteed to bring the group closer together! People drop out and watch the fun as they fail to find a place to stand. Work it down to one small island. (Best with large groups, juniors through adults.)

Snowstorm. Number the participants of the group by threes, fours, fives, or more, depending on the size of the group. There should be at least six or eight of each number. Form a double circle, gents in the inside circle facing clockwise, ladies in the outside circle facing the opposite direction. When music begins, all march single file around center, holding up the number of fingers representing his number and shouting the number while attempting to find a partner of the opposite sex with the same number. When a partner is located, the couple promenades around the hall counterclockwise in the original circle. Other couples join them. Extras remain in the center until the next exchange. Gents are then instructed to reverse direction and leave their partners. Mixer is resumed from the beginning. This may be continued several times, and then couples asked to keep their partners for the next game. (Best for large groups, junior highs through adults.)

Musical Handshakes. Double circle of couples with gents on the inside facing the ladies on the outside. When music begins (or other signal), gents move single file in one direction around the circle and the ladies in the opposite direction. When the music stops, each person faces the first person he finds in the opposite circle (any extras should go to the center to locate a partner and return to position as quickly as possible), shake hands, learn names, and follow the leader's instructions about a topic of conversation. Music plays again and everyone moves to find a new partner and game continues.

Each time before the music begins the leader instructs those in one circle to perform a stunt for the new partner when they have met and learned names. Another instruction is given the next time for the opposite circle. Possible instructions: describe a spiral without motions, drive a car without words (only motions) or use only words, describe an accordion without motions, tell whether you prefer a safety razor or an electric razor, preach a sermon by reciting the letters of the alphabet, preach a sermon only with the use of hands, etc. (30 or more players—best for large groups, senior highs through adults.)

Article Exchange. Double circle of couples with gents on the inside facing the ladies on the outside. As music plays, circles move in opposite directions. When music stops, each person faces a new partner, shakes hands, says "howdy," and exchanges some article with the other person (ring, shoe, pocket knife, pencil, watch, etc.). Anyone without a partner should go immediately to the center of the circle, find one, and return to the edge of the circle and complete the activity. Start the music again and continue the mixer until four or five articles have been exchanged, making certain that each player gives something of his own each time, not something he has collected. At this point, have everyone return each article to its owner. (Can be done with small or large groups, junior high through adults.)

Variation: The first time new partners meet they exchange right shoes, remember the name of the person from whom they received the shoe, and carry the shoes in their hands. Exchange left shoes the second time. Exchange both shoes and names the third time. At the completion of the fourth march, shoes are returned to their owners.

Promenade Mixer. Have couples promenade counterclockwise to good march or square dance music. Leader calls out "Gents forward five," "Gents back ten," "Ladies forward three," and so on. The circles move as indicated on each call and new partners get acquainted as they promenade and await the next call. Continue unti each participant has met a number of new people. This mixer may b combined with other mixers such as "Squat," "Snowstorm," and "Musical Handshakes." (Junior highs through adults.)

"Hello, Ladies." Double circle of couples with gents on the inside facing the ladies on the outside. Everyone sings. On the first line o the song, "Hello, Ladies" ("Goodnight, Ladies"), shake hands with partner. Everyone moves one person to his left and shakes the hand of the next person on the second "Hello, ladies." Everyone moves one person to his left again and shakes the hand of the next person on the third "Hello, ladies." Again everyone moves left to face anothe partner, and, on "We're going to leave you now," shakes hands Partners now clasp hands and skip or promenade around the circle while singing the chorus, "Merrily we roll along . . ." Stop and repeat action on second and third verses—"Have fun, ladies" and "Glad you're here, ladies" or work out other verses to fit the occasion Ladies may sing "gentlemen" rather than "ladies." Keep the las partner for the next activity. (Senior youth and adults.)

Waltz Mixer. This can be done to any old-fashioned waltz tune such as "Beautiful Ohio" or "Missouri Waltz." Arrange the group in a double circle formation with the gents on the inside facing the ladies on the outside. Practice the following actions before playing the music:

Clap own knees three times.

Clap own hands three times.

Clap partner's right hand with your own right hand 3 times.

Clap partner's left hand with your own left hand 3 times.

Clap your own knees once, own hands once, partner's hands once.

Repeat last line.

Clap own hands and count 1-2-3-4-5-6 (move to your left and face a new partner).

Repeat above sequence and move again to a new partner.

The directions may be simplified as follows: knees, knees, knees, hands, hands, hands, right, right, right, left, left, left, knees, hands, both hands, change-2-3-4-5-6. (Youth and young adults.)

Song Scramble. Select several songs which are familiar to the group. Write each line on a separate slip of paper. Give each player one of the slips. Instruct the guests to locate those who have other

parts of the same song, arrange the lines in the proper order, and sing
t as soon as they can. The groups can then be moved into the next
activity or asked to use the same songs to create a skit or prepare a
pecial rendition of their selection. (Youth and adults).

Variation: Song titles may be used in a similar way. Prepare slips
of paper in advance with familiar song titles written on them, the
ame number of slips of paper for each title to keep sections the
ame size. Instruct the participants to sing their songs as they move
round and find others with the same song.

Game Mixers

Choo Choo Train. Single circle of participants with at least two
or three extras in the center. No partners required. Before beginning
he mixer, rehearse a brief rhythm with the feet: left—, right—, left,
ight, left (two slow kicks followed by three quick ones). Each
person should take a little jump in place and extend the foot indicated when he comes down. Rehearse two or three times.

On the signal to begin, each player in the center goes to someone
on the edge of the circle, takes both hands in his hands, asks his
name, and repeats the name as both perform the rhythm with the
footwork (Jane—, Jane—, Jane, Jane, Jane). The person in the center
urns around to face the center of the circle, the person he met
places his hands on the first player's shoulder, and they move off
ogether to face someone else and repeat the procedure. The line will
continue to get longer and longer as the game progresses. Every time
a line meets a new person, all of those in the line should understand
what the new name is and repeat it together with the foot rhythm.
Every time this step is completed, all those in the line turn single and
face the center while the new person becomes the end of the line.
See which group can get the longest line! When everyone is in one of
the lines, have the lines join the ends of other lines and work back
into a big circle. (30 or more participants, junior highs through
young adults.)

Loose Caboose. Double circle of partners with both facing the
center, one standing behind the other with a firm grip on the other's
waist. The player in front is the "engine" and the one in the back is
the "coal car." In the center of the circle are two or more loose
cabooses (players working alone), depending on the size of the
group. The object of the game is for the loose cabooses to attempt to

attach themselves to the rear of one of the trains—that is, grab the waist of a "coal car." When this is done, the loose caboose becomes a coal car, the coal car becomes an engine, the engine becomes a loose caboose, and the game continues. Players are asked to remain in the large circle and not get out of position, although they can twist and turn all they want to prevent the loose caboose from attaching himself. This can be a rough game! (Any size group from juniors through young adults.)

Numbers Mixer. Begin with the group in a single circle formation The leader calls a number, such as "5", and the participants immediately re-form in groups of five. Another number is called (or whistle blown the number of times desired) and participants re-group again. The confusion is enough to make it fun if the group is kept moving rapidly from one grouping to another. As players re-group, they may be asked to get acquainted, discuss a specific topic, sing a song, or play a game until a number is called for them to re-group again. (Juniors through young adults.)

Face to Face. Double circle of couples with partners facing. An extra player stands in the center of the circle and calls "Face to face," "Back to back," "Face to face," or he may call "All change." On "All change" everyone, including the center player, seeks a new partner. The person left without a partner then takes his place in the center and gives the commands. For variety, other commands may be given such as "Shake hands," "Pat each other on the head," "Squat," "Step on each other's toes," and so on. (Best for junior and junior highs but may be used with older groups.)

Barter. Prepare in advance one set of different colored one-inch squares of construction paper for each participant. Each set should include the same number of squares (8—10 in number), each square being a different color and with the same combination of colors in each set. Give one set to each participant. The leader has already determined the value of each square—green may be worth ten points, red eight points, yellow five points, and so on. The participants do not know the values. Instruct the players to begin exchanging the pieces of construction paper according to their own estimate of what they may be worth. After a period of play, stop the game, give the values for each square of paper, and find out who has the most points. (Senior youth and adults.)

Name Your Neighbor. Play with a small group seated in a circle of chairs or on the floor. If the group is large, divide it into several small circles of players. Pass a pencil or some other object from person to person around the circle giving the object a name, perhaps "elephant." The first player says, "I, *(name)* , pass this elephant to you, _____." The second player says, "_____ told me,_____, to pass this elephant to you,_____." and so on around the circle. The first or both names of the players are supplied for the blanks. Ask each participant to concentrate on learning all the names. Volunteers may be asked to give all the names of players in their circles at the conclusion of the game. (Youth and adults.)

Trio Mixer. Arrange the group into a row of couples facing each other about six feet apart, gents on one side and ladies on the other. If the group is large, have a number of similar formations. Place three chairs at one end of the row facing down and between the line of couples. Number "1" gent (gent at the head of the line near the chairs) sits in the middle chair and the first two ladies sit in the other two chairs. The gent has a hat on his head. The gent places the hat on the head of one lady and slides, runs, hops, or dances (whatever instructions may be given) down the line with the other lady. They take their places at the foot of the lines. The extra lady moves to the center chair, the next two gents sit in the other chairs, the lady places the hat on one of their heads, and goes down the row with the other. The game continues until everyone has moved down the line. This mixer can be made competitive when there are two or more lines. (Senior youth and adults.)

Name Tag Mixer. Single circle of players facing the center. No partners required. Each person takes off his name tag and places it on the floor in front of him (a shoe may be used if name tags are not provided). On the signal to begin, everyone begins walking single file in one direction around the circle. On a signal to stop, everyone stops by someone else's name tag. The tag is to be returned to its owner. Circle is resumed for the next activity. (Best for large unacquainted groups of youth or adults.)

Fun Around the Clock. Provide the guests with a large mimeographed clock face marked off into twelve segments and instruct them to exchange autographs with a different person for each segment. For example, "X" will have "Y" sign his clock at 5:00 o'clock and "X" will sign "Y"'s at 5:00 o'clock. In addition to getting each person acquainted with twelve others, this may serve as a means for forming couples for later activities. In a large group, after the clocks are filled in, it is fun to have them return and find certain persons who signed a specific space and carry out a particular conversation or perform a stunt. (20 or more participants, seniors through adults.)

Nicknames. At some time during the early portion of the party, perferably during the mixer period when participants may be grouped in small circles, ask each person to give his nickname. If anyone denies having one, let the rest of the group give him one. Everyone is to be called by this nickname during the remainder of the party. This is best for small groups where everyone can stand or sit conveniently in the same circle. (Youth and adults.)

Pencil and Paper Mixers

Name Hunt. Give each guest a card or a sheet of paper and a pencil. Ask each to print his first and last name vertically, from top to bottom, down the left hand margin of his card (or down the center depending upon the variation used). Instruct them to move around the room filling in their cards with names of those present that begin with the letters on the card (or having letters within the name). The object is to see who can complete his card first. The first three or four players to finish may be used to begin another game or for a stunt later in the party.

Examples:	Variation:
John	roJer
Oscar	jO hn
Henry	Harry
Nancy	jeaN
Davenport	roDney
Opal	jOhnson
Ernest	JanE

No one's name should be used more than once. First or last names may be used. Nicknames and middle names may also be used when the group is small.

Word Mixer. Prepare cards in advance with letters of the alphabet on one side, enough to have one for each guest. Include extra vowels and leave out J, Q, X and Z. Each person is provided with a card and instructed to form a group with two or more other players whose cards will form a word. Write the word on the back of each card and re-group to form another word. Stop the game at the end of a given length of time and determine who has formed the most words. (Best for large groups, senior high through adults.)

Family Musical Mixer. Ten chairs (more or less, depending on size of group) are placed at random around the playing area. Ladies (if present) are asked to sit in the chairs. A man is asked to stand behind each chair. To the right of each man stands another man and to the left stands another lady. Another guest sits on the lap of the lady in the chair. The lady in the chair becomes the mother, the person in her lap is the baby, the man behind the chair is the father, the male to his right is the son and the female to his left is the daughter. Each is given a card indicating his role and surname: "mother Smith," "father Smith," "son Smith," "daughter Smith," and "baby Smith." The group around each chair will be given a different surname—a different set of cards for each group. While music plays all participants have a brief period to move around playing area exchanging their cards with other players. At the same time, the leader removes one or more chairs. When music stops, everyone hurries to get reorganized around a chair with his new family. Anyone not finding a chair may be eliminated, turn in their cards and become spectators along with other members of their new family.

Suggestions: One set of family cards should be prepared in advance for each chair. Size of crowd will determine number of chairs. Where participants are well-acquainted, actual family names may be used. When new families organize, there should be some time to get acquainted, perhaps with the leader giving a topic for discussion (for example, "discuss your favorite desserts").

This is a traditional Scotch party game learned from C. Stewart Smith, a Scots folk dancer at the Stockton (California) Folk Dance Camp.

*****

Most of these mixers are directed toward large groups. Small groups can get acquainted faster, get into informal games quicker, and do not require as much of this type of activity. There are many singing games and folk dances which may also be used as mixers:

Circassian Circle, Patty Cake Polka, Teton Mountain Stomp, Working on the Railroad, Shoo Fly, etc.

The mixers shown in detail on the following two pages are examples of prepared pencil and paper mixers. "Human Bingo" may be arranged with 16 or 25 squares, depending on the size of the group. In either case, it is best for groups with no more than 50 participants. After the spaces are filled in with signatures each player tears his name off the sheet and deposits it in a box or hat. These are then drawn to play "Bingo." Those getting 4 (or 5) spaces in a row checked off first might stand and give their names.

"Let's Get Acquainted" can be used in many forms and adaptations. Include questions to fit the local situation. It is important that this mixer be introduced with considerable enthusiasm in order for guests to begin moving promptly.

CHAPTER VII

Games

Following are quite a variety of games. Some may be better with particular age groups, some may be used with any age group (sometimes with adaptations), and some may be used with all ages at once (family programs). It is important that the leader select games with regard to experience, ability, and interests of the group for which he is planning.

Slap Jack. Players stand in a circle clasping hands. One player is "It" and walks around the outside of the circle and tags another player on the back as he passes him. The player tagged immediately leaves his place and runs in the opposite direction from "It" around the circle. The object of both players is to get back first to the vacant place left by the player tagged. Whoever succeeds remains in that place while the other player becomes "It." The game is sometimes varied by having the players bow, shake hands, and say "howdy" as they pass on the opposite side of the circle. This may serve to slow their speed and prevent someone from falling.

Flying Dutchman. Similar to "Slap Jack" except that two players, with hands joined, are the runners outside of the circle. Instead of tagging a person on the back they tag the joined hands of two players. There are no partners since a player may have to run with his neighbor on either side. They may also be required to shake hands and say "howdy" as they pass. An excellent variation is to have couples change partners when they meet on the opposite side of the circle.

Fire on the Mountain. All the players except one form a double circle facing inward. Players pair themselves off and one stands behind the other. Those standing in front are "trees" and those in back are "rangers." The extra player, who is the "Chief Ranger," stands in the center of the circle "on top of the mountain." He begins clapping his hands and shouting "Fire on the mountain! Run boys run!" As he does this, the "rangers" begin running around the outside of the circle. When the "Chief Ranger" stops his shouting and clapping, he and the "rangers" try to get in front of a "tree." The player left over becomes the "Chief Ranger." There is now a new set of "trees" and "rangers" and the game continues. Players may need to be encouraged to move out from the center of the circle as they begin crowding in.

Three Deep. Arrange the players in a double circle of couples facing the center as in "Fire on the Mountain." Two extra players, one the runner and the other the chaser, are located outside of the circle on opposite sides. On the signal to begin, the chaser runs after the runner in an attempt to tag him. The runner may save himself by entering the circle and stopping in front of a couple making the line "three deep." The outer player, the "third man," becomes the runner and may be tagged. In the same way, he may save himself from the chaser by stopping in front of a couple. If the chaser tags the runner, the runner becomes the chaser. Although both runner and chaser may dash through the circle, they may not pause within it except when the runner stops in front of a couple.

Cat and Mouse. Players stand in a circle facing the center with one additional player on the outside, the "cat," and another on the inside, the "mouse." The circle of players join hands. One of these is selected to be the "door." The cat walks around the outside of the circle and stops to knock on the door, "Knock, knock." The door asks, "Who's there?" and the cat replies, "The cat." The door then says, "What do you want?" and the cat replies, "Is the mouse ready yet?" The door says, "No, the mouse will be ready in a few minutes." The cat walks around the circle again and knocks on the door, the conversation is repeated, and the door says, "Yes, the mouse is ready, come in," and opens the door (drops hands with one of his neighbors and leaves opening for the cat to enter the ring). The players raise their joined hands and the cat proceeds to chase the mouse. If the mouse is tagged, he becomes the cat and chases the other player. If the cat does not catch the mouse within a certain time limit, stop the game. The mouse joins hands with others in the circle. the "door" becomes the "mouse," the "cat" becomes the "door," and the "mouse" selects a "cat" for the next game. Play several times.

Lemonade. Divide the children into two groups and place the groups at opposite ends of the playing area. The members of one group decide on some activity—washing dishes, cutting the lawn, picking apples, etc.—and work out motions to pantomime whatever the vocation may be. When the group is ready it forms a line and approaches the second group, and the following dialogue takes place:

First group:	"Here we come."
Second group:	"Where from?"
First group:	"New York."
Second group:	"What's your trade?"
First group:	"Lemonade."
Second group:	"Show us some."

The first group proceeds with its pantomime and the second group attempts to guess what it represents. If any member of the second group shouts out the correct answer, the members of the first group run back to their position with the second group chasing them. If anyone is tagged before he gets back to his home position, he joins the other group. The second group now has its turn to work out some activity. If no one guesses the "trade," the first group has another opportunity to pantomime.

Slide Right. All players except one are seated in a tight circle facing the center. There is one empty chair. The extra player is "It" and stands in the center of the circle. To begin the game, he calls either "Slide right" or "Slide left." If he calls "Slide right," the player with the empty chair to his right must move into it. Each player moves to his right as the empty chair appears next to him. "It" attempts to get into the empty chair as it moves around the circle. He may call "reverse," "change," or "the other way back" at any time, and the direction of movement must reverse. When "It" successfully sits in the empty chair, the player who should have taken this chair goes to the center, becomes "It," and continues the game.

Variation: One group started the practice of "It" saying "Banana split" as a signal for everyone to move to a chair on the opposite side of the circle while "It" tries to get into a chair at the same time. The leader must slip one chair out of the circle at this point, and the player left without a chair is "It" for the next game. This variation prevents embarrassment for the slow player who cannot get into an empty chair. (An excellent game for juniors through adults.)

This Is My Nose. Players are seated in a single circle facing the center. The leader selects the color of some article worn by one of the players or some object in the room and says, "I see red," or whatever the color may be. Any player who thinks he knows what it is may raise his hand and be given an opportunity to guess the object. The player guessing correctly starts the next game.

Apples, Oranges, Peaches, Plums. Players seated in a single circle facing the center. Select a player to be "It." He stands in the center of the circle. There should be no empty chairs. Each player is assigned the name of one of the fruits—the first player is an "apple," the second an "orange," and so on around the circle. "It" calls out the name of one of the fruits and those having that name must exchange places. No one can return to the chair from which he came. At the same time, "It" tries to get into one of the empty chairs. The remaining player becomes "It" and the game continues. If he calls "Fruit basket turnover," everyone must move to another chair.

Rotten Egg. A traditional game from eastern Kentucky for kindergarten and early elementary age children. Players are seated on the floor or in chairs in an informal circle. An extra player in the center of the circle is the "storekeeper." An extra player on the outside of the circle is the "customer." It is important that these two players be older children or, better yet, young people or adults. The children are "eggs." Instruct each to decide what color egg he is and keep this information to himself. The following dialogue takes place.

The center of the circle is a grocery store and the storekeeper is at work. The customer approaches:

Customer: "Knock, knock . . ." (appropriate motions)

Storekeeper: "Who's there?"

Customer: "The devil."

Storekeeper: "Go home and wash your face and read your Bible." (the Devil goes through the appropriate motions)

Customer (returning): "Knock, knock . . ."

Storekeeper: "Who's there?"

Customer: "The angel."

Storekeeper: "Come in. What can I do for you?" (Ad libbing goes on, customer purchases some groceries, and the topic finally gets around to eggs.)

Customer: "I'd like to buy some eggs."

Storekeeper: "What color would you like?"

Customer: "Red." (or any other color)

The storekeeper now begins to tap "eggs' on their heads as he moves around the circle. If one of the players has the color selected, he says, "Peep, peep," when tapped on his head. He then moves to the center of the circle, sits on the floor, and clasps his hands under his knees. The customer and storekeeper hold him under his shoulder pits, one on each side, after asking him his age and swing him back and forth the same number of times as his years of age. If his clasped hands separate before the swinging is completed, he is a rotten egg and joins the storekeeper (sits in one area of the play space). If his hands remain clasped, he is a good egg and goes with the customer. Continue the game using same or different colors until a number of eggs are collected for both the storekeeper and the customer. The collected eggs are then given a stunt or game to perform—tug-of-war, relay, or some other competitive activity.

Going Camping. Players are seated in a single circle facing the center. The leader goes around the circle and asks each player to tell the group what he is taking on the camping trip—tent, flashlight, blanket, gun, food, fishing pole, bed roll, and so on. Duplication of items is not important, but everyone should try to remember the articles which have been selected. One player is selected to be "It" and stands in the center of the circle. He begins walking around the inside of the circle. As he walks, he says, "I'm going camping and I'm going to take a blanket, a hunting knife, flashlight, etc." As he calls out the different items, the players taking these articles get out of their chairs and walk single file behind "It." At some point in the game he shouts "Thunder and lightning" and everyone runs to a chair, including "It." The last player to sit in a chair becomes "It" for the next game.

This game can be adapted very easily for Christmas (or other occasions) by calling it "Santa's Bag" and have everyone select a toy or some article he might give someone for Christmas. "Merry Christmas" could be the signal to run to their chairs.

Chicken and Grasshopper. Players are seated in a circle facing the center. Players number off by two's or, when older groups play, are seated as couples. The "one's" are one team and the "two's" are another. Every other player is on the same team. An object representing the "grasshopper" (rolled newspaper, ball, etc.) is placed in the hands of a player on one team and another object representing the "chicken" is placed in the hands of a player of the other team a short distance away. On the signal to begin, the chicken chases the grasshopper. Only the members of the team with a particular object may pass it. Both objects move the same direction as the game begins; however, the chicken may be reversed at any time and chase the grasshopper in the opposite direction. If the chicken catches the grasshopper, a point is awarded the team with the chicken. If the grasshopper escapes capture after a time limit, the team with the grasshopper is awarded a point. Switch the objects to the other team and play again.

How Do You Like Your Neighbor? Players are seated in a single circle facing the center. They number off around the circle from "1" to the total number in the group. One player is selected to be "It" and stands in the center of the circle. He approaches a player in the group and asks, "How do you like your neighbor?" The player may answer "I like him fine" or "I don't like him." If he says, "I like him fine," everyone changes seats and "It" tries to get into one. The remaining player becomes "It." If the player says, "I don't like him," "It" then asks, "Whom do you like?" He answers, "I like 10, 15, and 2," or any three or four numbers. Those who have these numbers change seats and "It" tries to get into one. If "It" is successful, the player remaining on his feet becomes "It."

Poison. Place a milk carton, pop bottle, tin can, or some other similar object in the center of the circle. Players join hands in a circle around the object and attempt to push or pull one another over the object. Any player touching or knocking the object over is poisoned and drops out of the game. If two players let go of hands, both drop out. Continue play until one player is left. Can be rough! (10–20 participants, juniors through senior high youth.)

Barnyard. Hide peanuts or other small objects around the playing area. Divide the group into teams. Give the captain of each team a paper sack. Each team selects the name of some barnyard animal—dog, cat, pig, donkey, cow, etc.—and rehearses in noisy confusion what its particular animal says. On the signal to begin, the teams start the search for peanuts. Only the captain of a team may pick up a peanut and place it in the paper sack. If the other members of the team find a peanut, they must emit the call of their animal to bring the captain. Count the peanuts when the game is ended to determine the winning team. (20 or more participants, juniors through young adults.)

Variation: Different objects may be hidden for each team—different colored candy kisses, different colored pieces of construction paper, different colored paper pumpkins to fit a Halloween theme, etc.—and each team looks only for the object assigned to it. Another interesting variation is to have each team join hands with the captain at one end of the line as they look for their treasure.

Musical Elbows. Similar to "Musical Chairs." Gents (or ladies) form a line in single file one behind the other. Players in the line alternate extending right and left elbows to the side. For example, the first player may extend the right elbow, the second player the left, the third player the right, and so on down the line. While music plays, ladies (or gents) walk in one direction around the line. When the music stops, each lady attempts to link one of her arms in one of the gent's elbows. Those who are unable to do so drop out. One or more gents are removed from the line and the game continues. Continue the game until one gent and one lady remain. This couple may be used to begin another activity or the ladies may now form the line.

Swat. Players seated in a circle of chairs facing the center. Place an overturned wastebasket or some flat object about a foot high on the floor in the circle. One chair is empty. "It" is provided with a rolled newspaper (have extra rolls ready).

"It" walks around the circle with the newspaper in his hand and swats someone, preferable on the legs. (Younger groups may have to be cautioned not to hit too hard!) "It" must then place the paper on the wastebasket and seat himself in the empty chair before the player hit can stand, pick up the paper from the wastebasket, and hit "It." If the player is successful in hitting "It" before he returns to his seat, the player also must replace the newspaper on the wastebasket and get back to his chair before "It" can pick it up and hit him. So it goes until one of the two players gets to a chair. The one remaining on his feet is "It" and the game continues. If the newspaper rolls off the wastebasket and onto the floor, the player who was hit may pick it up and run after the person who swatted him. A better strategy, however, is to leave it on the floor and force the other player to return and place it on the wastebasket even though the player he swatted is standing over him waiting for the chance to pick it up. Here is where the game gets exciting! (10 to 20 participants, an exciting game for young people).

Square Relay. Arrange the chairs in a square, the same number of chairs on each side of the square, facing the center. An empty chair is placed in the center of the square. If there are extra players, they may sit in empty chairs in the center and exchange with other players between games. Each side of the square is a team competing with the other three sides. Provide the player on the right end of each line with a small object (penny, bean, marble, etc.). All four objects should be identical.

On the signal to begin, the object is passed to the left along the line. Each person is required to receive and pass the object. When the last person in the line receives it, he stands, runs around the center chair without touching it, and back to the right end of his own line. In the meantime, everyone in his line has moved to his left leaving the first chair (at the right end of the line) empty. The runner seats himself, passes the object to his left, and the relay continues. All lines start at the same time and the first line returning to original seating arrangement wins a point.

This game has been played with as many as 200 participants with 50 chairs on each side of the square. It is more interesting, however, to divide into smaller squares and increase the competitive spirit. In small groups this game can be played several times, in large groups only once. (Any size group, juniors through young adults).

Indianapolis Speedway. Players seated in a circle of chairs facing the center or around a table. The game becomes more interesting if there are two or more groups competing with each other. Select one player in each group to be the "starter." On the signal to begin, the "starter" says "zoom" (to represent a car passing), the next person quickly adds "zoom," and so on around the circle to complete one lap. Move the "zoom" around the circle as fast as possible. See how long it takes to do 2 laps, 3 laps, 6 laps. Groups may be instructed to stand and let out a yell when they have completed the required laps. The winner can be determined in this way. Some groups have enjoyed varying this game by using sound effects of a 1930 car, "putt, putt, ah-ooga," or a future car with jet propulsion, "psssst." Work up other variations!

My Father Bought a Dog. Players seated in a circle of chairs facing the center or around a table. Provide one player in the group with a pencil or pen or some other object which is designated as a "dog." He turns to the player on his right and says, "My father bought a dog." The second player replies "A what?" and the first person responds "A dog" and hands him the "dog." The second player now turns to the player on his right and says, "My father bought a dog." The third person responds "A what?" and then the second person turns again to the first player and says "A what?" The first player says "A dog" to the second player and the second player says "A dog" to the third player and hands him the "dog." The third person now turns to the player on his right and continues the game. Note that the "A what?" must be relayed to the first player each time and the "A dog" relayed back. Continue the game around the circle. The game may be further complicated by supplying the person to the left of the first player with an object which is designated as a "cat" which moves in the same manner in the opposite direction around the circle. A group must be "on its toes" to complete this version around the circle. (Best for small groups of 8–15, junior highs through young adults.)

Variation: The response "What did it say?" may be used instead of "A what?" and "Woof-woof" instead of "A dog."

One Frog. Players seated in a circle of chairs facing the center of the usual formation, although this game can be played around tables or in other informal situations. The game becomes more interesting if there are two or more groups competing with each other.

One player starts by saying "one frog," the next player says "one head," the next "two eyes," the next "four legs," the next "in the pond," and the next "ker-plunk." The sequence is frog, head, eyes, legs, in the pond, ker-plunk. The next player in the circle then says "two frogs," and the game continues around the circle with "two heads," "four eyes," "eight legs," "in the pond," "in the pond," "ker-plunk," "ker-plunk." Note that a different player says each "in the pond" and "ker-plunk." Allow time for each group to practice and make sure it understands the sequence. See which group can go through "five frogs" first with no mistakes and no one helping anyone else. Any player making a mistake starts over again with "one frog."

Animal Exchange. Players seated in a circle of chairs facing the center or around a table. Instruct each participant to select the name of some animal and a motion which may be associated with that animal. For example, a skunk might be indicated by holding the nose, a cow by index fingers pointing up from each side of the head to indicate horns, a giraffe by extending an arm into the air with the hand bent to represent the head, a bird by flapping both arms like wings, a monkey by scratching the ribs, an elephant by extending an arm to represent the trunk, and so on. Each player has a different animal. Go around the circle once or twice to make sure everyone is familiar with all the motions represented in the group.

One player starts the game by doing his motion and then doing someone else's motion. The person with the latter motion then does his own motion and another player's motion, and so on. Anyone delaying a motion or making a mistake ends that series and the game is started again.

The game may be complicated (and made more interesting) if the motions are assigned to the chairs of the players selecting the motions rather than to the players. The leader is at the head of the circle and the player to his left is at the foot of the circle. When a person makes a mistake, he goes to the foot chair, everyone moves up one space as far as the empty chair, and everyone who moves takes on the motion which is assigned to that chair. Everyone attempts to get to the head chair or as close to it as possible. (Best played in small groups of 8–15; an exciting game for junior highs through adults.)

Menagerie. Players seated in a circle of chairs facing the center. Select one player to be "It." He stands in the center of the circle. He moves slowly around the circle, stops, and suddenly points to one of the seated players, and calls out a name such as "goat." The player to whom he points places a hand under his chin and bleats like a goat. The players on each side of him must supply one horn of the goat on the side of the head of the person to whom "It" pointed. The last player to perform his action exchanges places with "It" and moves on to point to someone else. Other possibilities folllow:

Elephant–The player to whom "It" points forms the trunk by extending clasped hands in front of him, players on each side form an ear at the side of his head with bent arms.

Seal–The player to whom "It" points barks like a seal, the players on each side clap hands.

Kangaroo–The player to whom "It" points forms pouch with his hands in front of him, the players on each side jump up and down.

Spirit of '76–The player to whom "It" points imitates the flag bearer, the player to his right becomes the drummer, the player on his left plays the fife–or the person on each side may become the drummer and second players on each side of him become fife players.

Firecracker—The player to whom "It" points says "sssst," the player on each side of him says "bang," and the second players on each side place their hands over their ears.

Start with one action and gradually add the others as the members of the group become more proficient. In a large circle several "Its" may be in the center at the same time. Create your own variations. (Older juniors through adults)

Wink. A good game for young people where the number of boys and girls is fairly evenly divided and the participants are well-acquainted. Start with the girls seated in a circle of chairs facing the center. There is one empty chair. A boy stands behind each chair, including the empty one, with his hands behind his back.

The boy behind the empty chair winks at one of the girls. She attempts to move quickly out of her chair and into the empty chair without being tagged by the boy behind her. He tries to tag her on her shoulder before she can get away. If she is tagged, she remains where she is and the first boy must try again. If she is not tagged, she moves to the empty chair and the boy who now has the empty chair does the winking. Play for a few minutes and then let the boys be seated and the girls do the winking.

Rhythm. Players are seated in a circle of chairs facing the center. The leader sits at the "head" of the circle and the "foot" is at his left. The chairs are numbered from "1" at the "head" on through the number of players in the group. Many rhythms are used for this game, some of them very fast. One is suggested here which most groups can use without too much confusion: everyone slaps his knees, claps his hands, and snaps his fingers in rhythm with the rest of the group. The leader can keep the group together by repeating "knees, clap, snap; knees, clap, snap" and so on until the action is synchronized.

To begin the game, the leader gets everyone into the rhythm and then calls the number of a chair other than his on one of the snaps. All numbers must be called at the time the fingers are snapped. The person whose number was called must call another number on the next snap. This continues until someone fails to call a number or does so out of rhythm. In this case, he moves to the "foot" chair, and the other players move up one chair as far as the empty chair. All those who move take on the number assigned to the chair into which they move. Everyone attempts to get to the "head" chair or as close to it as possible. Whoever is in the "head" chair begins the next game. (6—30 participants, junior highs through adults.)

Variations: (1) Instead of using numbers, tell a story around the circle, each player giving the next word on the next snap. A player breaking the rhythm starts the next story.

(2) Use word association. First player calls out any common noun or descriptive adjective on the first snap, the next player gives the first word that flashes across his mind related to that word on the next snap, the third person associates his word with the word of the second person, and so on. For example, the first player may say "house," the second player "yard," the third player "flowers," and so on.

(3) Use names of people in the group.

(4) The first player gives a category such as "cars." The names of cars must then be given around the circle on each snap.

(5) The first player calls out a letter of the alphabet, the second gives a word beginning with that letter, the third another letter, the fourth a word beginning with the letter just given, and so on.

In the Manner of the Adverb. Players are seated in a circle of chairs facing the center. Select one player to leave the room. While he is out, the members of the group choose an adverb such as "quietly," "happily," or "quickly." Keep the adverbs simple while learning the game. The first player is called back into the room. He approaches any player and asks him to perform some action in the manner of the adverb such as "Brush your teeth in the manner of the adverb" or "Walk in the manner of the adverb." Give him three guesses to determine what the adverb is. He selects a volunteer to leave the room for the next game. (10—25 participants, junior highs thorough adults.)

I'm Thinking of a Word. Players are seated. No particular formation is required. One player starts the game by saying, "I'm thinking of a word that rhymes with _____." He has a particular word in mind and uses another word with which it rhymes. Words should be of one syllable. He may, for example, say "light." Any other player who thinks he knows what the word is raises his hand. The first player recognizes him and he says "Is it?" and pantomimes what he thinks the word is. If he is wrong, the first player says "No, it isn't sight" or "No, it isn't night." When a player doing the pantomiming is correct, he answers, "Yes, it's fight." The player guessing correctly starts the next game. (Juniors through adults.)

Teakettle. Players are seated in a circle of chairs facing the center. Select two players to leave the room. While they are out, the two players decide upon two or more words which sound alike but are spelled differently (for example: pear, pair, pare). They return to the room, stand in the center of the circle, and begin a conversation in which they use the word "teakettle" instead of the chosen words (for example: "He teakettled a teakettle of teakettles" instead of "He pared a pair of pears.") At any time a seated player guesses what the words may be (he may whisper to one of the two for verification), he joins those in the center and gets into the conversation. He does not divulge what the words are. Play for two or three minutes or until everyone guesses the words. Select two more players to go out for the next game. (10–30 participants, junior highs through adults)

Here are some possibilities: flu, flew, flue; see, sea; deer, dear; sense, cents; to, two, too; seem, seam; red, read; stair, stare; mien, mean; vale, veil. There are many others. One couple came back to the group with "paradise" and "pair o' dice"! The members of the group can suggest some possibilities while the two players are out of the room.

Buzz. Players are seated in a circle of chairs facing the center. One player starts counting with "1", the next player says "2", and so on around the circle. Any player who has a number with "7" in it or divisible by seven calls out "buzz" instead of the number. Any player making a mistake starts over again with "1". Play to see how far the group can count without making a mistake or to a certain number, perhaps "50." (10–25 participants, junior through adults.)

Variations: (1) In addition to "buzz" use "fizz" for numbers which have "5" in them or are divisible by five.

(2) Use "buzz" for numbers with "7" in them or divisible by seven. Whenever a player says "buzz," the preceding player must say the next number, and then the numbers progress in the original direction again. For example, if the seventh player says "buzz," the sixth player says "8", the seventh player "9", and so on.

(3) Number "7" and those numbers divisible by seven (14, 21) are designated by clapping the palms of the hands together rather than counting the number. Those numbers with "7" in them but not divisible by seven (17, 27) are designated by clapping the backs of hands together. Whenever hands are clapped, the direction of the counting in the circle is reversed. For example, numbering starts to

the right, the player with "7" claps the palms of his hands together instead of calling the number, and the counting now moves to the left. No coaching allowed. Start over again each time a mistake is made. The procedure is complicated if the leader designates a different player to start with "1" each time a mistake is made. Object of this variation is to count to "30." It is not easy! Most groups will get into trouble when they get to "27" and "28."

Question Proverbs. Players are seated in a circle of chairs facing the center. Select one player to leave the room. The group agrees upon a well-known proverb. Distribute the words of the proverb among the players. The first player gets the first word, the second player the second word, and so on. If there are more participants than there are words in the proverb, repeat the words for the additional players. The player sent from the room returns to the circle. He proceeds to ask questions of members of the group. Neither the questions nor the answers need to make any particular sense, but the player answering the question must include his word in his answer. The player in the center of the circle listens carefully for repeated words and for key words included in proverbs. He gradually puts these together and works out the proverb. He may be allowed a specific number of guesses. Repeat the game with another player leaving the room. (8—20 participants, junior highs through adults).

Who's the Leader? Players are seated in a circle of chairs facing the center. Select one player to leave the room. The group decides upon a leader. The whole group starts clapping and continues until the player sent out returns and stands in the center of the circle. It is his task to discover who is leading the group in its actions. The leader changes the action from clapping to patting his head, twiddling his thumbs, patting his foot on the floor, or other obvious actions. He should change the actions as frequently as possible. The group follows his leadership and tries to avoid revealing who the leader is. It is amazing how quickly the action changes and how difficult it sometimes is to discover the leader. When discovered, the leader goes out and a new leader is selected. It adds to the fun if the game is played to music. (10—30 participants; an excellent game for juniors through adults.)

Ghost. This is a popular game with many youth groups. It is usually played in a circle but can be played in other situations—in a car, on a hike, sitting in the front room of a home, and so on. Select player to start the game. He begins by announcing a letter of the alphabet. The next player must add a letter to the previous one which will help form a word but not complete it. The third player adds a third letter, and so on. The first three letters do not count but, beginning with the fourth letter, if a player adds a letter which completes the word, he loses the game and becomes a "G," the first letter in "Ghost." For example, if the first three players give the letters "S", "H", and "O" and the fourth player adds "E", he becomes a "G". When he loses a game, each player must add an additional letter to form the word "Ghost." When any player becomes a complete "Ghost" he may no longer participate in the game and the other players ignore him. A complete "Ghost" may heckle the group by talking and questioning the players. If any player answers the Ghost, he is penalized by receiving the next letter in "Ghost" as he would if he completed a word. A player may challenge the person who preceded him if he doubts that the letter the player used will help form a legitimate word. If the challenger is correct, the preceding player recieves the next letter in "Ghost." If he is not correct, the challenger receives the same penalty. (Youth and adults.)

Circle Relay. Players are seated in a single circle facing the center. They number off by two's. All the "one's" are on one team; the "two's" on the other. Two adjoining players, a number "one" and a number "two," are each given a ball (rolled newspaper or other object which fits in with the theme of the party). On the signal to begin, the "one" ball is passed around the circle in one direction with only the "one's" handling the ball while the "two" ball is passed in the opposite direction with only the "two's" handling the ball. Players may interfere with the progress of the ball of the opposite team but they may not leave their chairs or grasp the ball with their hands. The team whose ball completes the circle first is declared the winner. Vary the game by changing direction or trying for two or more times around the circle.

Up Jenkins. Seat the players along both sides of a long rectangular table, with the same number of players on each side. Each side selects a captain. Provide a coin for one side of the table. This side places its hands under the table and passes the coin back and forth until the captain shouts "Hold." The player holding the coin retains it for the next action. On the command "Up Jenkins," elbows are placed on the table with hands clenched in the air. On the command "Down Jenkins," all hands are slapped to the table palms down. The members of the opposite side listen for the sound of the coin hitting the table and indicate to their captain where they think the coin is. Only the captain may request that a hand be raised. When the coin is found, the side with their hands on the table scores as many points as there are hands left with palms down. Give the coin to the other side and continue the game. (Juniors through adults.)

Chair Relay Series. This series of games has proven successful on many occasions. It may be used very well with some changes for any age group from juniors through older adults. While it can be adapted to any size group, it is most usable with 20—30 persons participating.

Arrange two lines of chairs facing each other about ten feet apart with an equal number of chairs on each side. If you have an odd number of players, one chair may remain empty on the short side or the player may serve as a judge. There should be space at the ends and in the back of the chairs for possible running space.

The activity involves the two lines competing with each other in a number of events which are brief in length and which follow each other rapidly to maintain variety and interest. The leader stands at one end of the lines of chairs and instructs the group. He tells them to move as quickly as possible when he gives instructions and to see which line can get it done first. He asks them to change sides immediately and as soon as they get seated to let out a yell. Then follows a series of activities (some suggested below) with the "changing sides" thrown in frequently. Arrange the order of events to keep them interesting. Don't have similar activities following each other. Don't try to use all of the following on the same occasion. Be selective and work out some of your own.

Flipping coin (or rolling a die)—one team is "heads" and the other "tails" (or "odd" and "even"). Flip coin. A team raises its right hands the first time its side comes up, left hands the second time, right foot the third time, left foot the fourth time, and the game is won when their side comes up the fifth time.

Passing life saver or ring on a toothpick held in the mouth.

Passing piece of paper on the ends of straws by suction.

Bouncing ball and passing to next person who does same thing. (On these passing games the stunt can be continued on down the line, then the objects involved passed directly back to the first person, the first team completing being the winner.)

Unrolling a ball of twine down the line and rolling it up again.

Unrolling a ball of twine and each person wrapping it around his waist.

Electricity with squeezing hands or tapping shoulders. (While hands are clasped, or when twine is wrapped around each person, try changing sides! It can be done!)

Provide each side with rope loop and have each person climb through it as it goes down the line. (Elastic works well.)

Pass armful of balloons down the line.

Each team lines up heel-to-toe to see which line has the biggest feet.

Casing and uncasing pillows.

Hold feet and ankles together and pass potato from person to person while holding the potato on both feet.

Number off each line by two's. Have all two's change sides with person opposite them. Everyone will still belong to his original team. Now throw a ball down the line and back again. It must go to each member of the team which means it will be thrown across to the other side and back again as it progresses down the line.

Give each person a balloon and have him blow it up and tie a knot in it. The first person in each line runs around the back of his chairs, down the middle to his own chair, and sits on his balloon and pops it. As soon as it pops, the next person starts, and so on until one side wins.

Many of these may be modified or adapted in different ways, and one can make up more of his own. Take a look at some of the equipment you have around you, at the group with which you will be working, and put them together in some new activities.

Activities with Balloons

Chariot Race. This is an excellent game for adults but may be used for younger groups. Pair off about a dozen of the biggest men in the group. Ask each to stand side by side with his partner with elbows linked to hold them together. This is the team of "horses." The smallest women in the group, one to each pair of horses, get behind the men and clasp their free hands. The women become the drivers of the "chariot." Each chariot has a different-colored balloon assigned to it. These balloons may be lying anywhere on the floor in the playing area. There should be the same number of them for each chariot.

On the signal to begin, players attempt to stamp on and burst the balloons of their opponents and, at the same time, protect thei letting go of hands or elbows. After complete instructions are given large paper bags are placed over the heads of the "horses" to preven their seeing where they are going—the guiding is left entirely to the women. Members of the audience may cheer for their favorite chariot. If teams have been in use during the party, these same teams may send out representatives to be the horses and the driver.

Balloon Hockey. Players are seated in two rows of chairs facing each other about 12–15 feet apart. There should be the same number of players in each line. Number the players from "1" on one end of each line on through the total number of players in the line Place a large cardboard box on its side with the opening toward the playing area for a goal at each end of the lines. A balloon and two brooms (paddles, sticks, or some other object for batting) are placed on the floor in the center of the playing area. The leader calls a number and members of each team with that number run for a broom and begin to swat the balloon toward the box at the left end of their lines. A point goes to the team for each success. If the game goes beyond a short time limit, another number should be called and those players with the new number exchange places with those batting the balloon.

Variation: Provide each person with a rolled newspaper and call two or more numbers at a time. Watch the fun!

Balloon Sword Fight. Played by 5 or 6 players at a time, who may be representatives of the teams. Each participant plays for himself. Provide each player with a long "airship" balloon to the end of which is scotch-taped the head of a sharp tack. A specific playing area is outlined. (Players should not have too much space in which to battle.) Each player holds the opposite end of the balloon with one hand.

On the signal to begin, players attempt to burst the balloons of their opponents with the tack on the end of their balloons and, at the same time, prevent their own balloons from being at "tack"ed. When the balloon of a player is burst, he must drop out of the game. The last player to survive is the winner.

Balloon Stomp. Participants play as in the previous game, or small teams may compete against each other. Each contestant is provided with a round balloon and a piece of string about a yard ong. Instruct the players to inflate the balloons, tie a knot around the neck of the balloon, tie one end of the string to the inside of the knot, and tie the other end of the string to their ankles.

On the signal to begin, players attempt to stamp on and burst the balloons of their opponents and, at the same time, protect their own. No holding is allowed. A player drops out when his balloon bursts. The surviving player or team is the winner.

Balloon Swat. Same as above except that the round balloons are tied to the rear of the belts of the players, or around their waists, and each player is provided with a rolled newspaper. They attempt to swat the balloons and break them and, at the same time, protect their own.

Balloon Gambit. The group is divided into two teams. Provide a large inflated baloon. One team acts as the defenders and the other the destroyers. The defenders try to protect the balloon by batting it into the air and keeping it away from the destroyers; the destroyers try to burst it by grabbing it or stepping on it. When the balloon has burst, another one is put into play and the destroyers become the defenders. If score is kept, the minutes taken to burst the balloon are counted.

Balloon Pick-Up. A number of beans are scattered on the floor. Provide each player with an inflated balloon which he must keep batting into the air with one hand while he picks up beans with the other. If the balloon touches the floor, the player is eliminated. The winner is the one who collects the largest number of beans. If several players succeed in remaining in the game for too long a period of time, call time and declare the participant who has the most beans the winner.

Baloon Basketball. Seat players in two lines of chairs (or on the floor) facing each other so that the knees of participants on opposite sides are no more than a foot apart. There should be the same number of players on each side. An extra player is seated on each end, about two or three feet from the end of the line, holding his arms out like a basketball hoop.

```
            XXXXXXXXXX
    O                        X
            OOOOOOOOOO
```

The leader drops a balloon into the center of the line. The players in each line attempt to bat the balloon to their left and into the hoop at the left end of their line while attempting to prevent the opposite team from doing the same in the opposite direction. Use only one hand to bat the balloon. Players must remain seated. The arms serving as hoops at the end of the lines must remain steady and not move to meet the balloon. A team receives a point for each success. If the lines are long, use several balloons along the line at the same time. Play for a time limit or a certain number of points. After playing the game as described above for a while, slip in a balloon filled with helium and watch the fun!

Balloon Fortune. Participants are asked to write fortunes on small slips of paper which are rolled and placed in balloons by inserting, inflating, and tying at the neck. These may be used in a variety of ways: decorations (place in buckets or barrels, hang from ceiling or wall, etc.); party starters, mixers, games (check these activities and work out ways to adapt); other balloon activities above; musical games (passing balloons around circle or group as music plays—when music stops, each person keeps the balloon he has); etc. At some point, everyone has a balloon other than the one he prepared. Participants are asked to stomp on, sit on, or pop the balloon in some way and keep the fortune. These are shared with others.

Hints for the Recreation Leader with Children

Less social contact is recommended with younger children than with older ones. Many kindergarten and younger elementary age children are ready for limited social activity, but they should not be pushed too rapidly into group play. Social activities should be balanced with individualistic play such as crafts, art, playing with books, playground activities, nature walks, roller skating, wading, etc.

The younger the child, the shorter the span of attention. The leader and those planning recreational programs for early elementary age children should recognize the need to progress from one simple activity to another rather rapidly. There are some exceptions but the interest of this age child in a specific activity usually is short.

The younger the child, the less equipment is needed. Children can be depended upon to use their imagination and should be encouraged to do so. Generally they feel more freedom in expressing themselves than do older people. Dramatic activities, storytelling, and rhythms are appropriate.

The younger the child, the less muscular coordination is present. Early elementary age children are not yet ready to play organized sports although some adaptations may be used.

Allow the children to play at their own level. Adult leaders only serve to complicate the situation at times. Activities should be informal, the children should be at ease, and opportunities for sharing should be provided.

Give each child the opportunity to participate at his own speed and, if the program allows it, give each of them the chance to be out in front of the group. Every child wants to be "It" for a game. Select children who catch on quickly to start a new game but do not ignore the slower ones.

When it is necessary to have an "It" for a game, use some indirect means for determining this player to avoid showing any favoritism. Rhymes, such as the following, may be used:

Engine, engine, number 9
Running along Chicago line
Please tell me the correct time
1, 2, 3, 4, 5, 6, 7, 8, 9, 10, 11, 12

The leader starts by pointing to any child in the group and then moves around the group pointing to a different child on each word. The child to whom he points on the last word becomes "It."

All children, especially those who do not usually get enough attention at home or elsewhere, require honest praise for something well done. Compliment the child on his achievements but do not make him an example or a "teacher's pet."

Use democratic processes with the group. Children enjoy sharing their thoughts and ideas. Leaders will find the children making spontaneous suggestions if they know they have the freedom to do so. Some might even have a new game which the leader can add to his file.

If there are "disturbed" children in the group, avoid overcompetitive games. Encourage activities where everyone takes the same role with no children being placed in possibly embarrassing situations. Do not force a child too fast. Be objective—not emotional. A good balance of individualistic activities may help this situation.

Do not use prizes if competitive games or relays are introduced.

Help the children to play the activity for the thrill and satisfaction o the experience.

Play good games. Do not play them too long or too often and stop while everyone is still having a good time and move on t another.

Play with the children. They will be glad you did, and so wil you.

Have fun! The children will, too.

Progressive Games Party or Carnival Night

Progressive Party

Name _____

Start at Game No. _____

Follow rules at each game.

Score according to score chart at each game.

GAME NO.	SCORE	GAME NO.	SCORE
1.	_____	6.	_____
2.	_____	7.	_____
3.	_____	8.	_____
4.	_____	9.	_____
5.	_____	10.	_____

TOTAL SCORE _____

If any ????, ask committee members wearing a red ribbon

Possible use for Progressive Games Party:

1. Family Nights
2. "Starter" for many parties
3. Informal game room activities
4. Home Fun—Try some with your family, especially on rainy days!

Suggestions for Progressive Games Party:

1. Have "mood" music such as marches or circus records in background.

2. A fortune teller booth always adds to the program.

3. Have committee members circulate around room to help traffic keep moving (pace setter).

4. Avoid the following: equipment made of glass, sharp objects, candles if against fire regulations, ball bounce games if there is any chance of damaging walls or windows.

5. If progressive party games are used for a whole evening, include some type of closing activity for the whole group, such as stunts, songs, or folk dances.

Following is an example of instructions which can be left at each game for the participants to read:

No. 1
BALL BOUNCE
10 Trials

Bounce ball over chair into basket

One point for each success

Some games which might be used:

Bounce ball into waste basket.

Bounce ball over chair and into waste basket.

Roll tennis ball between milk cartons.

Toss paper plate through wire hoop (stretched coat hanger) suspended from the ceiling.

Drop clothes pins into milk bottle from back of a chair.

Walk a chalk line while looking the wrong way through binoculars.

Toss milk bottle tops into a muffin pan.

Bounce ball on floor, against wall, and catch in a funnel.

Roll golf ball through paper towel tubes.

CHAPTER VIII
Fun with Musical Movement

Big Circle Mountain Square Dancing

Music: Any good hoedown

Big Circle Square Dancing has been danced for many years and is truly our own American Dance. The important thing to remember is that it has come to us by way of people who have enjoyed dancing and being together. The dance is simple enough for everyone to enjoy it; yet even in its simplicity, it is beautiful to watch.

To the Caller

Enjoy the dance yourself.
Demonstrate the figures early in the evening.
Call from the floor, if possible.
Call loud and clear. Keep it simple.
Call in rhythm with the music.
Keep one jump ahead of the dancers.

To the Dancer

Listen to the caller and the music.
Use a smooth walking shuffle (please, no hopping, skipping or jumping steps).
Remember, it takes team work.
Enjoy the calling, the music, and especially the fellowship of your fellow dancers.

The Big Circle Dance consists of two basic formations—Big Circle Figures and Small Circle Figures. A dance is usually put together in the following manner:

1. OPENING—Big Circle Figures
2. BODY—Small Circle Figures
3. CLOSING—Big Circle Figures

For the Big Circle Figures or opening and closing figures, eight or more couples form a single circle, hands joined, man with his partner on his right. The lady on the man's left is his corner lady. From this formation, any of the calls listed as Big Circle Figures may be danced.

Small Circle Figures, or the body of the dance, are figures done by two couples dancing together. These couples have been designated as odd and even couples before the dance begins, by counting off beginning with the lead gent counterclockwise around the ring.

As you design your Big Circle Dance, keep in mind the following sample pattern:

Opening or Big Circle Figures

Circle left
Circle right
Single File, Lady in the lead
Grand right and left
Swing
Promenade
Queen's Highway
King's Highway
Circle left
Circle right

Body or Small Circle Figures

Odd couple out to the even couple
Birdie in the Cage
Odd couple on to the next
Birdie in the Cage

Closing Big Circle Figures

Promenade
Circle left
Circle right
Make a basket
Swing
Promenade
London Bridges
Promenade
Swing

Description of Figures

Big Circle Figures

Circle Left—

Dancers join hands, man with his partner on his right, and the dance to the left.

Circle Right—

Dancers join hands, man with his partner on his right, and the dance to the right.

Single File, Lady in the Lead—

Single circle with gent's partner in front. Dance counterclockwise around the circle.

Grand Right and Left—

Single circle of couples, partners facing, man counterclockwise ladies clockwise. Partners join right hands, pull by, passing right shoulders, then join left hands with the next person, pull by, passing left shoulders. Continue right and left around the circle until the original partner is met.

Swing—

Partners face and assume ballroom dance position. Each takes one step to the left, walks forward around each other. This is known as *walk-around swing.*

Promenade—

Couples facing counterclockwise, lady on man's right. Man extends right arm across the back of partner's shoulders to take her right hand in his right hand above her right shoulder. Left hands are joined in front of man's left shoulder. In this position, dance around the circle, counterclockwise. This is known as a *courting promenade* or *over-the-shoulder promenade.*

London Bridge—

From a promenade, the lead couple reverses direction, gent holds ng partner's right hand with his left hand, to form an arch over the heads of the other dancers. Each couple in turn follows the couple in front. When the lead couple reaches the end of the line, they turn and duck under the arches, followed by the other couples, until they re back to the head of the line and then promenade.

Queen's and King's Highway—

From a promenade, the lead lady turns right, leaving her partner, and dances in the opposite direction around the circle followed by he other ladies in succession. When she meets her partner, she promenades with him. *King's Highway*—the lead gent steps out behind his partner, turning right, to follow the lady immediately in front of him in opposite direction around the circle. Each successive man follows him out, around and back to his partner for a promenade. (Gent steps in behind his partner from the promenade.)

Roll the Ladies In—

From an over-the-shoulder promenade position, keeping hands joined, ladies do a left face turn ending up on the inside of the ring (to her partner's left).

Roll the Ladies Out—

Ladies do a right face turn back to place, gents assisting in the same manner.

Shoo Fly Swing—

Lead couple out the middle of the ring,
Turn your partner right—then left at the ring,
Back to the middle with a right hand swing,
Back with a left to the outside right.

The lead couple moves inside the circle and swings partner with a right hand around. The lead lady leaves her partner and turns her corner with a left hand around, returns to partner with a right hand around, and continues left to next gent and right to partner. When first couple begins figure with the fourth couple, the number 2 man takes his partner and begins the right and left reel. Each couple continues the figure until they are back home. *(Note:* while in the middle of the circle, gent turns no other lady but his partner.)

Basket—

Promenade
Ladies to the center and circle left,
Gents keep going, circle right,
The other way back
Gents stop to the left of partner
Raise hands and make that basket
Ladies bow, gents know how,
Circle left and away you go.
Reverse the basket and away you go,
Break and swing your partner.

Ladies drop hands with gents, move toward center of circle, join hands and circle to the left. Men join hands and circle right. Reverse circles, men going left and ladies right. Gents stop to partners' left raise joined hands over ladies' heads and in front of ladies' waists. Circle continues to move left. Men raise hands over ladies' heads and back to place while ladies raise joined hands over mens' heads and behind their backs. Circle continues to move left. Break and swing partners.

Small Circle Figures

Odd Couple Out to the Even Couple

Odd couple out to the even couple,
Circle left, now the other way back.

Single circle of couples, numbered off or having been designated odd or even before dance begins. Odd couples move out to couple on the right, join hands and circle to the left. Reverse circle, move back to position.

Right Hands Across—

Right hands across and howdy do,
Back with the left and how are you?
Gents join right hands, ladies join right hands and walk forward.
Reverse direction, joining left hands.

Duck for the Oyster—

Duck for the oyster, dive for the clam,
Duck right through and roll it around,

Circle left, once around,
Swing your opposite lady,
Swing your own.

Hands joined with even couple, odd couple ducks under arch formed by the even couple and back to place. Even couple dives under arch formed by odd couple and back to place. Odd couple ducks under arch again, odd gent drops right hand (this is the only hand hold that is broken), odd gent goes left, odd lady goes right, pulling even couple through under their own arms. Circle left once around, swing the opposite lady, then swing partner.

Take a Little Peek—

Circle to the left, circle to the right,
'Round that couple and take a little peek,
Back to the center and swing your sweet,
'Round that couple and peek once more,
Back to the center and swing all four.

Circle left, circle right. Odd couple separates, peeks at each other around the even couple. Return to place and swing partner. Separate and peek once more, back to place and both couples swing partners.

Birdie in the Cage—

Circle to the left, circle to the right,
Birdie in the cage, six hands around.
Birdie hop out and crow hop in,
Six hands up and you're gone again.
Crow hops out and hops on a limb,
Circle to the left, you're gone again.

Circle left, circle right. Odd lady moves into the middle of the circle, six hands joined around her, circling left. Odd lady moves back into her position in the circle while odd gent (crow) moves to center of circle. Gent moves out to position and all circle left.

Four Leaf Clover—

Circle left and back to the right
Odd duck right under for a four leaf clover and turn on over
Odd arch and even go under
Circle left
Swing your opposite lady

Now swing your own.

Circle left, circle right. Even couple makes an arch. Odd couple ducks under arch and turns away from each other, passing their joined hands over their own heads to form the clover leaf. Odd couple arches and even couple ducks under and all circle left. Swing the opposite lady, then swing your partner.

Chase that Rabbit—

Circle to the left, now back to the right,
Chase that rabbit, chase that squirrel,
Chase that pretty girl around the world,
Chase that 'possum, chase that 'coon,
Chase that big boy 'round the room.
Circle to the left,
Swing your opposite, then swing your own.

Circle left, circle right. Odd lady leads out, in between the even couple, around and behind the even lady, back between the even couple, around and behind the even gent, odd gent following all the way. Then the odd gent leads out, following the same pattern with the odd lady chasing behind. Circle left, swing the opposite, swing your partner.

Basket—

Circle to the left and back to the right,
Eight hands across,
Ladies bow, gents know how,
Circle left
Break and swing your opposite
Now swing your own.

Circle left, circle right. Men reach across joining hands. Ladies join hands under gents. Men raise hands over the ladies' heads and ladies raise hands over the gents' heads, forming a basket with hands joined at waist level. Circle continues to move left throughout figures. Break and swing your opposite, swing your partner.

Ladies Chain—

Circle left and back to place,
Two ladies chain,
Chain them over and chain right back,

Swing your opposite, swing your own.

Ladies move to the center, joining right hands and passing by. Lady joins left hands with the opposite man, who places his right hand in the small of her back, and moving forward turns her around to place. Ladies chain back, turning to place in the same manner with partner. Swing the opposite lady, swing your partner.

Little Girl Step Through—

Circle to the left and back to the right.
Little girl step through
Little boy, too,
Swing the lady on the right,
Circle to the left and back to the right,
Little girl step through
Little boy, too,
Swing your partner.

Circle left, and back to the right. Drop hands. Men and opposite ladies join right hands, ladies step through the circle passing left shoulders, continue walking as men step through circle passing left shoulders. All join hands and circle clockwise. Gent swings lady on his right, puts her on his right and circles left, then circles right. Repeat entire figure, ending up swinging with original partner.

Traffic Jam No. 1—

Music: Any good polka
Formation: Random—i.e., wherever people are standing.
Purpose: To get people moving without partners—loosen up to music.
   1. Stamp foot three times
   2. Clap hands three times
   3. Walk four steps in any direction
   4. Repeat 1—3
   5. Slide (sashay) eight slides to the left (Foul to bump into anyone.)
   6. Slide (sashay) eight slides to the right
      Repeat as many times as desired.

Traffic Jam No. 2—

Music: Any good polka

Formation: Two people facing each other anywhere in area. May be male-female combination but two females or two males together is fine.

Purpose: To dance with a partner having to dodge others on the floor.
1. Stamp foot three times
2. Clap hands three times
3. Turn partner with a right elbow four steps around
4. Repeat 1—3
5. Join both hands with partner and slide (sashay) eight slides to gent's left
6. Slide (sashay) eight slides to gent's right
    During 5 and 6 it is a foul to touch another couple while sliding.

Tiptoe Bingo—

Music: Bingo RCA No. 416172
Formation: Hands joined in a single circle. Large groups may choose to have circles within circles.
Purpose: Sing along while dancing and follow the leader.
Action:
1. Circle left 16 steps while singing, "A little black dog sat on the back porch, and Bingo was his name." Repeat.
2. Circle right 16 steps singing, "B-i-n-g-o, B-i-n-g-o, B-i-n-g-o and Bingo was his name."
3. Tiptoe in four steps, one step on each letter of B-I-N-G. Back out with hands raised on O. (Everyone follows the leader's action during this part of the action, i.e., tiptoe to the singing of the letter B . . . tiptoe on right toe, I . . . on the left toe, N . . . tiptoe on right toe, G . . . tiptoe on left toe, O . . . all raise hands and back out to original circle.)

Suggestion to leader: During No. 3, the leader should vary the action of movement. Hop in, bend over while going in, take big giant steps, go in backwards, etc. If the group is old enough, participants may be given the responsibility of leading the group in.

Nine Pin Square Dance—

Music: Any good hoedown
Formation: Four couples in a square set. One extra person in the middle, thus the name *nine pin.*

Purpose: A good mixer of people. Strickly a fun dance.
Action:
Opener:
   Circle left and circle right
   Swing your partner
   Promenade partner home
Figure:
   Couples one and three go forward and bow to the nine pin and back out to place.
   Couples two and four go forward and bow to the nine pin and back out to place.
   Couples one and three go forward and circle left around the nine pin, then circle right and back to place.
   Couples two and four do the same.
   Nine-pin swing number one, swing number two, swing number three, swing number four (if a girl is in the middle, she swings gents, if a boy is in the middle, he swings girls.)
   Nine pin and all the same (girls if the nine pin is a girl, boys if the nine pin is a boy) join hands and circle left.
   Break and swing—grab a partner. The one left out goes to the center and becomes the new nine pin.
   Promenade partner around the ring to home position.
   Repeat three more times.
Closer:
   Circle left and circle right
   Swing partner and promenade home.
   All bow to the nine pin and thank them for the dance.

Imagination Dancing--

Music: A variety of styles, tempos, moods, etc.
Formation: Participants can be anywhere in any position. Seated at tables, standing, etc.
Purpose: Have people move to music without having to worry about doing it right. Whatever they do is right. This is especially good for helping boys who don't want to dance. They can hit a home run and run the bases without being shy.
Action:
   Leader calls out an action and the group carries out their interpretation of the action in time to the music being played.

Examples for leader: Try catching a football high in the air (music light and lively)
Bounce a ball with big bounces
Chase a butterfly with your hands
Scoop up a balloon from the floor and bounce it in the air
Run to the music
Hop over cracks

Clap Rhythm—

Music: Beer Barrel Polka or any good polka
Formation: Standing, in no particular formation
Purpose: This is an excellent activity for the beginning of a party with a large group.
Action:
　　Ask each person to turn and face another person near him. Make sure everyone has a partner. Teach them the following clapping rhythm: slap own knees, clap own hands, clap partner's hands, and clap own hands (done to a 1-2-3-4 count). Add music when the rhythm has been learned. It may be done with the group singing "Working on the Railroad," although singing makes the activity too difficult for some groups.
　　When this has been worked out successfully, ask each couple to get together with another couple in a tight square with partners opposite or "kitty-corner" from each other. Each couple determines whether it will be couple number one, beginning on the first beat, or couple number two, beginning on the second beat or one beat later. Add music. When this has been worked out, ask each foursome to get together with another foursome and form a tight circle. Ask each person to pair off with the person opposite him. This may be worked out by asking each group to count off by fours. Those with the number one will become partners, those with number two are partners, and so on. Partners with number one begin on the first beat, those with number two one beat later, those with number three on the third beat, etc. Practice and then add music.

Three Blind Mice—

Music: "Three Blind Mice" sung by participants
Formation: Squares of sixteen players with four players on each side of square.

Purpose: This activity demands group coordination which proves to be a challenge to many participants.
Action:

Form the players into squares of sixteen players with four players on each side of the square. The number of participants in each line is not important—if necessary to include everyone in the activity, extra players may be added to some of the lines. Walk through the activity first. Ask each line to do a right face and face the right end of the line. Walk eight steps forward in the line of direction, about face, walk eight steps in the opposite direction and face the center of the square when back in the original positions. Walk four steps in and four steps backward. Turn single, in position, with four steps and face the center of the square again. Clap hands three times. Practice two or three times to make certain everyone understands the action.

Ask the group to sing "Three Blind Mice" once. Then perform the action while singing. Ask the group to sing the song as a four-part round with each line taking one of the parts. Perform the action as a round. Try the round one more time in silence with the players mouthing the words.

I've Been Working on the Railroad—

Music: I've Been Working on the Railroad" sung by participants
Formation: Double circle of couples, facing counterclockwise, inside hands joined, with ladies to the right of the gents.
Action:

The following steps will be done four times as the song is sung through once—8 walking steps beginning with the left foot, heel and toe step with left foot, heel and toe step with the right foot, and two knee-bends. On the second knee-bend everyone raises his free hand and shouts "Hey!" On the last line a "Toot, toot!" may be substituted for the "Hey!" At this point the gents move ahead one position, get a new partner, and the song and actions can be repeated.

The "Dinah, won't you blow" portion, which is often added to this song, may be included. If so, the following actions are used—partner's hand is released and gents step in front of partners to form a single circle facing counterclockwise. All place right hands on right shoulders of person in front and march around singing. Left hands move freely to demonstrate movement of wheels of train. When the imaginary cord is pulled for the "Toot," all gents step forward to join a new partner—the one directly in front. (When this part is used, gents do not advance until this point.) Repeat from beginning.

Bibliography

Each of the following books has an excellent section on Big Circle Dancing:

And Promenade All by Helen and Larry Eisenberg, Tennessee Book Co., Nashville, Tennessee, 1952.

World of Fun by R. Harold Hipps and Wallace E. Chappell, Division of the Local Church, Board of Education, The United Methodist Church, Nashville, Tennessee.

The following books deal specifically with Big Circle Dancing:

The Appalachian Square Dance by Frank H. Smith, Berea College, Berea, Kentucky, 1955.

Bascom Lamar Lunsford, "Minstrel of the Appalachians" by Pete Gilpin and George Stephens, The Stephens Press, Asheville, North Carolina, 1966.

The following records are excellent resources for Big Circle dance music:

Educational Activities, Inc., Record Numbers 45-107 ("Boil Them Cabbage Down"/"Little Liza Jane"), 45-108 ("Lonesome Road Blues"/"Mountain Dew"), AR 52 ("Big Circle Mountain Square Dancing"), AR 53 ("Appalachian Clog Dancing"), AR 54, ("Appalachian Mountain Folk Songs"). P.O. Box 392, Freeport, N.Y., 11520.

Dance Record Center, Record Number LP 36 ("Big Circle Mountain Square Dance Music," Stonycreek Boys and G. Bannerman). 10 Fenwick St., Newark, New Jersey, 07114.

World of Fun, Division of the Local Church, Board of Education, The United Methodist Church, Nashville, Tennessee.

✳
CHAPTER IX
Mental Teasers

Activities in this category, depending upon difficulty, challenge, and the situation in which used, are effective with all age groups, including family programs. They may be used to begin a party, as part of a party, as the entire party, entertainment at dinner meetings, when some people are hanging around with nothing to do, in a car or bus on trips, and in other situations.

For the Young and Not So Young

The following activities have been used frequently with older elementary aged groups but, in some cases, may be readily adapted for younger or older groups:

The Moon Game. Players are seated in an informal circle. The leader draws a moon with his *left* hand, saying at the same time, "I draw a moon, two eyes, a nose, a mouth." The next player tries to draw the moon in the same way and so on around the circle to find out how many players have discovered the trick. The catch is drawing the moon with the *left* hand.

Stir the Mush. Players are seated informally in a circle. The leader has a stick with which he will "stir the mush." He goes through the motions of stirring the mush as he says, "Down in Florida we stir the mush this way. See if you can do it the same way. *Now watch me.* I stir the mush, I stir the mush, and I stir the mush." The stick is passed to the next player in the circle and he tries to do it the same way the leader did. The trick is that he must be sure to include "Now watch me" in what he says.

Whoops, Tommy. Players are seated in an informal circle. The leader starts the activity by pointing to his fingers as he says "Tommy (pointing to little finger), Tommy (ring finger), Tommy (middle finger), Tommy (index finger), whoops (runs his pointing finger down the valley between index finger and up the thumb),

Tommy (points to thumb). Now do it like I did." He then *folds his hands* in his lap. The next player then tries it and so on around the circle. The trick is folding the hands in the lap.

Pass the Scissors. Players are seated in a single circle. The leader has a pair of scissors. He passes these to the player next to him, saying either "I pass them crossed" or "I pass them uncrossed." The next player accepts the scissors and may say "I received them uncrossed and I pass them uncrossed." The game continues around the circle. Players are told by the leader, or anyone else who knows the trick, whether they are right or wrong while others try to figure out the solution. Whether the scissors are "crossed" or "uncrossed" has nothing to do with the scissors. The trick lies in whether the player's legs are crossed or uncrossed.

Going to Minneapolis. This is an accomplice game in which the leader has a partner who is in "cahoots" with him. The partner leaves the room and, while he is out, the group selects the name of any city in the United States. The partner returns and the leader asks him, "Are we going to Nashville?" or any other city. The partner answers "no." The dialogue continues until the leader asks the question and includes a two-word name such as St. Louis or New Orleans. The partner then knows that the city will be the one included two questions later—it will be the second city following the first two-word city. Members of the group may be allowed to leave the room and try it when they think they have found the solution. This game can be made more complicated and almost impossible to solve by having a prearranged rule that the first time the answer will be the first city named after a two-word city, the second time it will be the second named, the third time the third named, and then back to the first.

Teasers for the Not So Young

The following activities are particularly usable with youth and adults (from junior highs and older) but, in some cases, may be adapted for younger groups:

Turkish Numbers. This teaser is best done with a table but may be done on the floor. The leader needs four objects with which to make the numbers—pencils and pens are particularly effective, but other objects such as silverware, coins, sticks, or whatever is handy may be used.

The leader may tell a story such as the one which follows: "One time while I was in the Air Force we were making a flight over Turkey. We had engine trouble and were forced to land near a small village. While we were there waiting for repairs to be made on the airplane, we were taught by the natives to make Turkish numbers. This is the way they did it."

The leader proceeds to place the four objects in different formations on the table and asks the players to guess what the numbers are, any number from one to ten. The members of the group are asked to look for a pattern in the formations as different numbers are revealed. The players are not to reveal the trick when they become wise to it. They can be called upon to give the number when others are unable to guess it. Actually, the formation of objects has nothing to do with the number. After each pattern is formed, the leader places a number of his fingers on the edge of the table. These fingers represent the number, not the objects on the table. It is always surprising how many people never notice the fingers but continue to try to work out some system in the pattern of objects. Numbers higher than 10 may be worked out by raising the hands from the edge of the table and replacing them to form additional numbers.

Magazine Magic. Place nine magazines on the floor or table in the following formation:

x x x

x x x

x x x

While the leader's partner is out of the room, or, better yet, hides his eyes, the leader or players select a magazine; for example, the magazine in the upper left-hand corner of the formation. When the partner returns, the leader points to any one of the magazines but is careful to point to the upper left-hand corner of whatever magazine is the first one to which he points, indicating to the partner that the magazine selected is in the upper left-hand corner of the formation of magazines. The partner gets the signal and continues to say "no" until the leader points to the selected magazine. If the upper right-hand magazine was selected, the leader will point to the upper right-hand corner of the first magazine to which he points. The position to which he points on the first magazine lets the partner know which magazine has been selected. Members of the group try to figure out how the partner knows which is the magazine chosen. Rather than allowing them to give the answer when they have learned the trick, ask them to leave the room or hide their eyes and try it.

Book Baffler. Participants are seated informally in a circle. The leader places a row of three piles of books in front of him on the floor or on a table. The number of books in each stack is not important. Three or four is a good number. The leader has someone in "cahoots" with him. This partner hides his eyes while the leader or the group selects a book. The partner opens his eyes, the leader begins pointing to the books, and the player in "cahoots" will know the book selected when it is pointed to. The group is to figure out how it is done. As in other mental teasers, ask them not to reveal the trick or ask questions. If a player thinks he knows how to do it, ask him to hide his eyes and try it.

The leader and his partner have the stacks of books named in their minds. The two outside stacks are "this" piles and the inside stack is a "that" pile. When the leader points to a book, he always says either "Is it *this* book?" or "Is it *that* book?" The key words— "this" and "that"—must correspond with the name of the stack for the book to be the one selected. If the leader points to a book in an outside pile and says, "Is it *this* book?", the partner knows it must be the book because it is a "this" pile. If the leader says, "Is it *that* book?", he knows it is not the right book because the key word does not correspond with the name of the pile. If the leader says, "Is it *that* book?", as he points to a book in the middle stack, the partner knows it is the right book because the words correspond.

Magic Money. Players are seated informally in a circle. The leader has a partner who is in "cahoots" with him. The partner leaves the room while the group selects a number. The group may choose any figure up to 155. Perhaps "52" is selected. The partner returns to the room. The leader indicates the number selected by using two coins of different values, perhaps a quarter and a dime. He places the quarter on the face of an imaginary clock on the floor or table and on a number that is to be multiplied by itself, or squared. In this case, the leader places the quarter on "7". 7 x 7 is 49. 3 more are needed to make "52" so the dime is places on 3 with the head side up to indicate that 3 is added. The trick could be done by placing the quarter on 8 which multiplied by itself is 64. The dime is placed on 12 with the head side down indicating that this number is to be subtracted. The answer is still "52." Let the members of the group struggle with this one for a while.

Swami. This is a mind-reading trick that works fine with a small group. Instruct each player in the group to write a simple question on a slip of paper, sign his name, fold it, and put it in a box or hat. Have an assistant pass the hat and stand beside the Swami. Also needed is a confederate in the group who does *not* put a question in the hat, but pretends to. The Swami takes a folded question from the hat and places it to his forehead. He concentrates, perhaps says some magic words, and then says "   wants to know if, etc." The name called is that of the confederate in the group, who acts surprised and says that he wrote it. The question given was manufactured by the Swami. The Swami looks at the folded question and hands it to his assistant to verify. He then goes through the same procedure again of drawing a slip of paper and holding it to his head. This time he uses the question that was on the first slip of paper. He is always providing the question which was included on the previous slip of paper and giving the impression of knowing it before he sees it.

Matching Game. Prepare a number of objects for display on a table or scatter them around the playing area. As each guest arrives give him a mimeographed sheet of clues which are intended to match the objects. The guests write the name of the article which matches the clue. Answers should not be shared with other guests. Give the answers to the clues before moving to another game.

The more unusual the clues the more interest is generated by the participants. Following are a number of suggestions. Do not use all of them at one time (ten may be sufficient).

The reigning favorite (umbrella)
Cause of the American Revolution (tacks on tea)
Bound to rise (yeast)
A place for reflection (mirror)
A rejected beau (ribbon)
Bound to shine (polish)
A drive through the wood (nail in wood)
Seen at a baseball game (pitcher)
A messenger (one cent)
A sower of tares (needle and thread)
An entertainment (ball)
Rib production (picture of woman)
Palm one and don't speculate (bird)

Fire when ready (match)
A letter from home (letter "O")
The Colonel (kernel of corn)
Our popular band (rubber band)
A perfect foot (ruler)
Headquarters (pillow)
A stirring event (spoon in cup)
The end of winter (the letter "R")
Pig's retreat (pen)
Where love is found (dictionary)
The peacemaker (scissors)
A year behind time (calendar behind clock)
A sound idea (horn or whistle)

Malaga Grapes.

Malaga grapes are very good grapes,
But Smyrna grapes are better.

The leader uses a pointer (broom handle, yard stick, tree branch, or some other) and points to the four points of the compass on the ground, floor, or table, beginning with North and moving to East, South, and West as he recites the above line. Participants take turns trying to repeat the action exactly as it was done by the leader. The trick to the activity is not in the pointing of the stick but a cough (clearing of the throat) by the leader just before the pointing is begun!

Ding-a-Lings. Following are three pages of "Ding-a-Lings" which may be copied on typing paper or poster board and posted on walls for guests to interpret, or a sheet of them may be mimeographed and used as a "party starter" or at some other point during a recreational event. Each picture or set of words represents a familiar phrase. Solutions are as follows:

Ding-a-Lings No. 1:

1. Sock in the eye
2. Pair of pants
3. Flat tire
4. Ring around the Rosie
5. Lone Ranger

 6. Safe on first
 7. Keep it under your hat
 8. Broken Engagement
 9. A little misunderstanding between friends
10. The worm turned
11. Circles under the eyes
12. Crooked lawyer
13. Right in the middle of everything
14. Far away from home
15. Mixed-up kid
16. Six of one kind and a half-dozen of another
17. No stone left unturned
18. Take one before each meal

Ding-a-Lings No. 2:

1.	Bowl of fish	7.	Square root
2.	Powder magazine	8.	Bits of wisdom
3.	Home on the range	9.	Sign of the times
4.	Heart attack	10.	See-Saw
5.	Slip knot	11.	Fast buck
6.	Tow truck	12.	Left bank

Ding-a-Lings No. 3:

 1. Two boys after the same girl
 2. Legal separation
 3. Girl with a million dollar figure
 4. Looking backward
 5. Money on the line
 6. A day off
 7. The forty-niners
 8. Nothing after all
 9. Tooth decay
10. Five degrees below zero
11. Outnumbered three to one
12. Repaired
13. Few and far between
14. One after another
15. Easy on the eyes

DING-A-LINGS (Well-known sayings)

1	2	3	4
O / I / S O C K (sock drawing)	PANTS / PANTS	TIRE	(G ℛ ROSIE) ∿

5	6	7	8
RANGER	SAFE / FIRST	YOUR HAT / KEEP IT	ENGAGE MENT

9	10	11	12
F R I E N D S STANDING MISS F R I E N D S	MAOW ƎHT	(two figures with o above)	ᴸAᵂᵧER

13	14	15	16
EVERY | RIGHT | THING	FAR HOME	D K 1	ONE KIND ANOTHER / ONE KIND ANOTHER / ONE KIND ANOTHER / ONE KIND ANOTHER / ONE KIND ANOTHER / ONE KIND ANOTHER

17	18		
ƎNOTS / ƎNOTS / ƎNOTS	TAKE ONE MEAL / TAKE ONE MEAL / TAKE ONE MEAL / TAKE ONE MEAL	Identify the well-known sayings in the spaces provided below —	

1.

2.

3.

4.

5.

6.

7.

8.

9.

10.

11.

12.

13.

14.

15.

16.

17.

18.

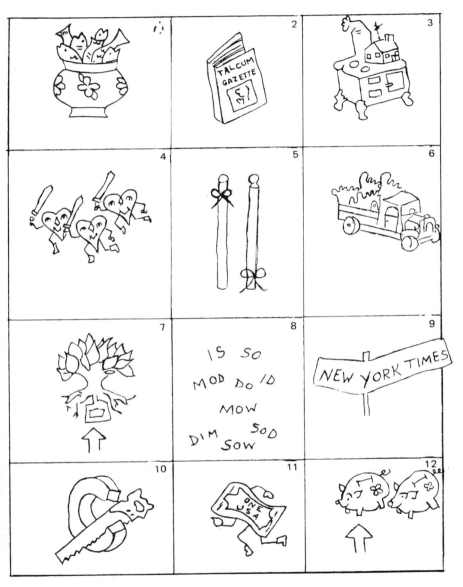

Instructions: Write in each square what the "ding-a-ling" picture message says.

WHAT'S THE MEANING?

1. GIRL–BOY–BOY

2. L E G A L

3. GIRL $1,000,000

4. GNIKOOL

5. <u>MONEY</u>

6. SUNDAY, MON., TUES.,
   THURS., FRI., SAT.,

7. RRRRRRR
   RRRRRRR
   RRRRRRR
   RRRRRRR
   RRRRRRR
   RRRRRRR
   RRRRRRR

8. A L L O

9. 2th DK

10. ___O___
    D.D.S.
    LL.D.
    Ph.D.
    M.A.
    M.D.

11. O U T
    3 2 1

12. RE RE

13. F–FAR–E–FAR–W

14. 11

15. EZ
    II

16.   G
                 N
               I
             H
           T
          Y
         R
        E
       V
      E

17. WETHER

18. WORL

19. BANGFF

20. BRILLIANT SURGEON
    BRILLIANT SURGEON

21. N
     E
      W
    THINGS

22. WOWOLFOL

23. SSSSSSSSSSC

24. S H I P

16. Everything going up
17. Bad spell of weather
18. World without end
19. Starting off with a bang
20. A couple of smart operators
21. A new slant on things
22. A wolf in sheep's clothing
23. Tennessee
24. Space ship

Penny Puzzle. ("A penny for your thoughts"). Take a Lincoln penny and see if you can find the following items:

1. A small animal (hare-hair)
2. A snake (copperhead)
3. A messenger (one cent-sent)
4. A flower (tulips-two lips)
5. Part of corn (ear)
6. Edge of a hull (brow)
7. A country (U.S.A.)
8. A fruit (date)
9. A part of a river (mouth)
10. A beverage (tea-"T")
11. Yourself ("I")
12. A building (temple)
13. What a ship sails on (sea-"C")
14. Two kinds of votes (Aye's and no's-eyes and nose)
15. Impudence (cheek)
16. Slang for hat (lid)
17. A student (pupil)
18. Result of victory (won-"one")
19. Strokes of whip (lash)
20. A book of the Bible (Numbers)
21. A policeman (copper)
22. Worn by work horse (collar)
23. A layer of paint (coat)
24. End of nail (head)
25. Doors have them (locks)
26. A hotel (inn-"IN")

CHAPTER X
Spoke Relays

Formations for spoke relays:

Arrange teams like the spokes of a wheel. The starting line for each spoke will be at the rim of the wheel. A touch base should be in the center of the circle (the hub of the wheel).
Purpose of formation:

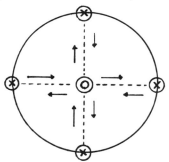

Each team has a viewing advantage not present with side-by-side relays. A sense of community involvement can be developed. Confusion as to who belongs in what line is eliminated. Spectators have a better viewing advantage. Any type relay may be used in this formation. Especially good for Fourth of July celebrations, large gatherings for picnics, etc.

Paper Bag Relay. Form teams with paper carton 20 feet in front of each team, and a pile of paper bags beside each team at the starting line. At the signal, the first player picks up a bag and runs to the carton, blowing up the bag. The player bursts the bag, throws it in the basket and returns to touch off the second player who repeats.

Block Head Relay. Players line up at starting line facing hub. Provide each player with a pine block or mill end. On "get ready," each player places the block on his head and locks his hands behind his back. On "go," the players start for the goal. If the block falls off, it must touch the ground. Players must stop, replace block, and put hands behind back before continuing. This can also be done with a bean bag on each shoulder and hands clasped behind back.

Catch, Throw, and Squat. Arrange the teams in lines at rim. Station the captain of each team 15 or 20 feet in front of his team, facing it. Mark a three-foot circle in which the captain must keep one foot. At the signal, the captain throws the ball to the first player who catches it, throws it back to the captain and sits down; the captain then throws over the head of the first player to the second player who repeats. Continue until all are sitting. Balls which the captain must recover by removing his foot from the circle count one point against the team.

Bow-Legged Relay. Divide the participants into teams and give the leader of each team a basketball. (Volleyball, large balloon, etc.) He must place it between his knees, and, on "go," walk to the hub and back to his line. Continue the race until everyone on one team has completed the procedure.

Message Relay. This relay calls for mental alertness more than physical ability. Place the captains at the hub opposite their teams. Give each captain a folded card on which a brief message is written. All cards contain the same message. At the signal the captains open the cards and read the messages. When a captain is sure he knows it, he drops the card on the floor, runs and gets the first player in his line, and returns with him—whispering the message to him on the way. When they reach the hub, the captain stays there and the first player goes back to get the second. Continue until all have run. When the last player of a team gets the message he runs to the leader who is stationed near the starting line, and states the message to him. Since the messages as stated are invariably far from correct, the team turning in the nearest correct statement is declared the winner. The captains should be cautioned to read the message carefully and deliberately before running. When the captains drop their cards the leader should pick them up. The players should be warned to run slowly and to pay attention to the message.

Pillow Case. A pillow in a case is placed on the floor in front of each team. The players compete in couples. At the signal, the first couple of each team runs forward, the man removes the pillow from the case and hands both to the lady who puts the pillow into the case again. They drop the pillow, return to the starting line, and touch off the next pair who repeat.

Shopping Bags. Give each team two large shopping bags. The first person in line puts his feet into the bags, runs to a chair, sits down, takes his feet out, and runs back to give the bags to the next person in line.

Folded Chair. The runner goes to a folded chair, lying on the floor. He picks it up, unfolds it, sits down, cracks his heels together three times. He folds the chair again, puts it back down on the floor, and returns to tap the next player.

Balloon Fan Relay. Take a large inflated balloon, place it on the floor, and fan it with a piece of cardboard or panelboard to the hub. Pick it up, carry it back, and give the balloon and board to the next in line.

Balloon Pop. Each contestant is provided with a seven- or eight-inch round balloon which has already been blown up and tied. On the signal to start, the first person in each line runs to the hub, places the balloon on the ground (or on a chair), and sits on it until it pops. He runs back to the rim and touches off the next person, who repeats. This continues, with the first team to finish being the winner.

Crab Race. Contestant crawls backwards on all fours to the hub, runs back to the line, touches off the next player who repeats. This continues, with the first team to finish being the winner. This race may be run also on all fours with the back of each contestant toward the ground. This is a good one for young boys.

Shoe Scramble. All shoes are removed from the players and placed in a pile, or left shoes in one pile and right shoes in another. On the signal to start, all run and find their shoes, put them on, and return to the starting line. First line with all shoes on feet wins.

One-and-All Relay. The first and second players in each team join hands. On the signal to start, they run to the goal line. The first player remains at the goal line while the second returns and clasps hands with the third player. These two run to the goal line, the second player remains, the third player returns to get the fourth player, and so on. The team that first transfers all its members to the goal line wins the race.

Bowling Relay. The first player in each line is given a ball, preferably a large one like a playground ball or volleyball. On the signal to start, he runs to the hub, turns, and rolls the ball back to the second player. The second player repeats the action and the relay continues until the entire team has moved to the goal line.

Back-to-Back Relay. Players on each team pair off and stand back to back with elbows linked. On the signal to start, the first pair runs to the hub and back to tag the next pair. One person is running forward and the other backward. Their directions reverse coming back.

Wheelbarrow Relay. Members of each team are paired off. The first pair in each line gets ready by having one member get down on his hands and knees while the second member grasps the ankles of the first person, lifting up much as he would the handles of a wheelbarrow. On the signal to start, the couple moves toward the hub with the man on the ground walking on his hands while the other holds up his legs and pushes him along. When the goal line is reached, the players exchange positions and return in the same way to tag the next couple.

Horse and Rider Relay. The players on each team pair off. One player in each pair becomes the horse and the other the rider. On the signal to start, the rider jumps on the horse's back and they run to the hub. Here they switch positions, the rider becoming the horse and horse the rider, and they return to their line and tag the next pair. This may also be done on all fours or on hands and knees.

Team Relay. On the signal to start, the first player runs to the hub, marked by a chair for each team, circles it, and runs back to the starting line. He then takes the next person by the hand and both run around the chair. They come back and get the next person, repeating the race until the entire team with hands joined runs the course. The first team to finish is the winner.

Over-and-Under Relay. The first player in each line is given a ball, beanbag, or some other object which can be handled easily. On the signal to start, he passes the object over his head to the second player, who passes it between his legs to the third, who hands it over his head to the next, and so on. When the object reaches the end of the line, the last person runs to the front and continues the relay. The relay continues until everyone has returned to his original position. Less complicated versions of this relay are passing the object over the heads or between the legs.

Crooked-Walk Relay. On the signal to start, the first player on each team places his weight on the left foot, swings right foot around behind the left and forward and puts his weight on it. He continues by returning the right foot to the ground and swinging the left foot around behind the right, continuing this movement until he reaches the goal. The goal line should not be far away. He runs back and tags the second person in line, who proceeds to the goal in a similar fashion.

Newspaper Relay. The first player in each line is given two half-sheets of newspaper or two stiff sheets of cardboard. On the signal to start, he moves toward the goal line without stepping directly on the ground; he steps on one sheet of newspaper, places the other in front of him, steps on it, places the other in front, steps on it, and so on. He may return either this way or run back to give the sheets of newspaper to the next person in line. Extra sheets of newspaper should be ready in case some are torn.

Tunnel Relay. On the signal to start, the last player begins to crawl between the legs of those in front of him to the head of the line and takes his place there standing. As soon as he has started, the next player follows. The first line whose members have all crawled through and stand in the original order wins the relay.

Measuring-Worm Relay. The first player in each line squats down at starting line and moves forward by walking on hands to a full-length prone position. Then he brings his feet up to his hands. Repeating this action he continues to the hub, jumps up, and runs back to tag the next person.

Hoop Relay. The first person in each line runs to the hub, where there is a hoop. This may be a hula hoop, a loop of rope or heavy string with ends tied, or a loop of elastic with the ends tied or sewn together. The player picks up the hoop, passes it over his head, steps out of it, and carefully replaces it where he found it. He then runs back and tags the next person in line, who repeats this action.

CHAPTER XI

Outdoor Games

No-Equipment Games

Sardines. This is "hide and seek" with a vengeance. The group stays together in one room or area while one or two persons go hide. After a given time, the whole group tries to find the ones who have hidden, but anyone finding them joins them in hiding, rather than announcing his find. This continues until all have found the original hiders, and the last one or two to find the group, which is usually packed like sardines, are the ones who hide next. Impress upon the searchers the need for absolute quiet when they join the ones in hiding, for giggling will reveal the secret.

Merry Mixup. The guests are divided into groups of ten to twenty persons, with a captain. The captain is taken from his own group to another one. Upon signal, the captains are to mix-up the group they are now in charge of, by weaving them around, in and out, over and under, while they have hands joined. When each captain is through with this, he goes back to his own group and at the signal begins to unscramble his own team.

Pinwheel. Six to fifteen people seated back-to-back in each of two or more circles, legs spread with feet touching neighbor's feet. The first person in each pinwheel starts at the same time and runs around his circle, stepping between the legs of the members of his team and sits down when he gets back to his position. The next person rises and does the same thing, etc., until each person has gone around once. The first team completed is the winner.

Shifty Lines. A square of four lines of people, any number in each line, with the tallest person at the left end of each line and the shortest at the right end. Leader in the center turns slowly and points to one side of the square. Number one team (each team numbered) must move to that side in same order and other teams in corresponding positions. The team getting in place first with hands up wins. (Best with fair-sized groups.)

Run, Sheep, Run. The players are divided into two teams, the "sheep" and the "hunters." A home base is selected. The sheep go out to hide and agree on certain signals which their leader may use. Some groups use colors for their signals. *Red* may mean "Keep quiet"; *blue*, "Move cautiously toward home base"; and *green*, "Get ready to run." The leader of the sheep returns to home base and accompanies the hunters as they start out to look for the sheep. Each group must remain together. He may call out the signals whenever they are needed. When he thinks the hunters are far enough away from home base, he shouts, "Run, sheep, run!" At this, both teams start running for home base. The first team back is the winner. If on the other hand the hunters sight the sheep, they start for home base and the leader immediately calls "Run, sheep, run!" The teams change sides and begin again.

Closing the Door. Players form a circle without joining hands. Two players are selected to stand outside the circle at opposite sides. On the signal to start, one player chases the other in an effort to tag him. The second player weaves in and out between the players in the circle as often as possible. Every time he passes between two players, they join hands and the "door is closed." The chaser may not go through this space. The person being chased attempts to close all the "doors" with himself on the inside of the circle and the chaser on the outside, or vice versa, to finish the game. When this is done, each picks another player to start the next game. If the person chased is tagged, he becomes the chaser and the game continues.

Duck, Duck, Goose. The game begins with a formation of players in a circle: they stoop over, facing the center. One player is "It" and stays outside the circle. "It" walks around the circle, tapping each player on the head and saying "Duck" as he does so. When he comes to the one he wishes to chase him, he says "Goose." That player immediately rises and chases "It" around the circle to the vacant place which he left. If caught, the same player is "It" again. If he gets to the vacant place safely, the "Goose" now becomes "It" and repeats the game.

Equipment Games

Beater Goes Round. All the players except one stand in a circle shoulder to shoulder with their hands behind them. One player goes around the outside carrying the "beater"—rolled newspaper, towel, or stocking filled with cotton. He puts the "beater" in someone's and and steps into that person's place after moving once around and outside the circle. The one who receives the "beater" begins to "beat" he person to his right. This person runs around the circle and back ome trying to avoid the beating as he is chased. The beater then goes round the outside of the circle and gives the "beater" to someone lse.

Stop Ball. A circle of players numbers off. The leader has a olleyball. He throws the ball into the air, shouting a number, and he person with that number tries to catch the ball on the first ounce, while all other players run away. When the player catches he ball he immediately yells, "Stop." All players stop and then take hree walking steps (usually three) from where they stopped, counting loud together. Here they must stand, and the player with the ball ries to hit a player below the shoulders. If the person is hit, he ecomes the next leader and throws the ball.

Old Plug. The group stands in a large circle and has a volley or layground ball. Three persons stand in the center of the circle in a ingle file line, holding on to each other at the waist. Old Plug is the ack one of the three, and members of the group try to throw the ball nd hit Old Plug. The three in the center try to keep Old Plug away rom the ball. When he is hit, the one who hit him becomes the head f the three, the former second man becomes Old Plug, and the origi- al Old Plug joins the circle.

Stride Ball. Players stand in a circle with feet spread apart (stride osition). Feet are touching each neighbor's and hands are on knees. An extra person who is "It" is in the center of the circle. The game egins by "It" placing a volleyball on the ground and batting the ball vith open hands across and/or around the circle, attempting to bat it etween a person's legs. Players must keep hands on knees until ball s batted in his direction, then the player bats the ball back into the ircle to keep it from passing between his legs. Ball must be kept on he ground at all times. Players are not permitted to bat ball while it s in the air. If "It" succeeds in making ball pass between a player's egs that person exchanges places with "It." Players may not stoop r put knees together to keep the ball from passing between legs.

Bottle Baseball. Layout as in softball with bases approximately 25—30 feet apart and bottles for bases (other objects may be used, of ourse). From 6—15 players form a team. The pitcher rolls volleyball o home plate. Batter kicks ball and goes around outside of bases and eeps going until he gets home. If the ball is caught on the fly by opposing team, the batter is out. Otherwise, whoever gets the ball throws it to first base where bottle must be tagged with the ball, the ball is thrown to second base and bottle tagged, etc. If the runner gets home first, he is safe. If the ball gets to a base before the runner, the runner is out. Other than these, the rules are generally similar to softball.

Four Square Ball. A court is prepared by scratching lines in dirt, chalk, or tape on floor, 16' by 16' divided into four equal squares which are lettered A, B, C, D. A smaller area may be used. One player stands at each square. Any number up to around 15 may stand in the waiting line. Object is for players to advance to square D and remain there as long as possible. A volleyball or playground ball may be used. The player at square D starts play. Standing at the corner of his square, he bounces the ball and then strikes it with either one or two hands or plays it directly from his hand directing the flight of the ball so that it bounces in one of the other squares. The player at the receiving square keeps the ball in play by striking it off the first bounce to one of the other three squares. Play continues until one of the players fouls or fails to return the ball properly. When this occurs, the offending player is eliminated and goes to the end of the waiting line. Players behind the offending player all move up one square. The waiting line's first player always moves into square A;

Rules: The ball must arch. If struck downward it is a foul. The server stands inside square D and gives a fair serve. A fair serve is one which bounces at least one foot. A player may go anywhere to return a fair ball—out of court or into another square.

Fouls: A ball that hits a line (any line). A ball struck with the closed hand (fist). A ball that hits a player while he is standing in his own square. The foul is committed by the player struck by the ball. If a player is outside his court and hit by a ball on the fly, the player that hit the ball has committed the foul. If two players persist in playing the ball only to each other, a rule may be added requiring a player to return the ball to another square than the one from which it was received.

x x x x x x x x x x x x x x (waiting line)

Corner Spry. Teams of 8 to 10 participants each. Players stand in position to form corner of room with one person "It" standing alone to form the last corner. Use volleyball or playground ball. "It" faces

1is team and throws the ball to the first person to his right. That
3erson returns the ball to "It," and he throws it to the second person
standing next to person just thrown to). He returns the ball to "It"
1nd play is continued until the ball is thrown to the last person (to
'Its" left). This person calls "Corner Spry," runs to "Its" position
1nd throws the ball to "It" who has run to the right to stand in the
'irst player's position. The new "It" now repeats. Continue until all
:he players have been "It" and all are in the original position. First
team to complete wins.

```
o  o  o  o  o
            o
            o
            o
   o        o
```

Kick the Can. Here is another old-timer played in many parts of
the country with a number of variations.

A small tin can (a No. 2 size is good) is placed in a small circle.
Another area is set aside as the prison. One player is selected to be
"It." Another player is selected to run and kick the can. When he
does so, everyone except "It" runs to a hiding place. "It" runs after
the can and returns it to the circle where he taps it on the ground ten
times as he counts out loud. Leaving the can in the circle, he begins
to hunt for the hidden players. If he identifies someone in hiding, he
calls the name of the person and runs back to the can and touches it
with his foot. That player then becomes a prisoner. A player who has
not been identified may run in while "It" is out hunting and kick the
can as far as he is able. Then prisoners are free to run and hide again.
"It" must retrieve the can and return it to the circle and count to ten
as before. If all the players are caught and placed in prison, the first
one identified becomes "It" for the next round of the game. Since
one person may remain "It" for a considerable length of time, a time
limit might be set, or some other means devised, to give other players
an opportunity to be "It."

French Cricket. This is an excellent outdoor game for a group of
fifteen to twenty-five people. It can be used with mixed groups but it
is particularly good for boys. A paddle and a tennis ball (or soft
rubber ball) are the only equipment needed. The paddle should be
about three and one-half feet long and shaped as follows:

The group forms a circle about thirty feet in diameter. One player is the center holds the paddle. The ball is thrown by one of the player in the circle, attempting to hit the player in the center below the knees. If he does so, he changes places with him. The center playe attempts to protect himself by hitting the ball with the paddle. He may not move his feet while someone has control of the ball. If he does so, someone may call him on it and change places with him. I the ball misses the center player or is hit with the paddle, some othe player retrieves the ball and continues the game by throwing from the edge of the circle. If someone catches a fly ball off the paddle, he changes places with the player in the center.

Stick-in-the-Hole. An adaptation of hockey, or shinny, is called Stick-in-the-Hole. (There should be definite rules about swinging the stick to avoid roughhousing and bruised heads and shins.) This game is played by six to twelve players in an open area with a radius o forty feet or more. (It has been played inside a building by using chalk circles for holes and adapting rules to this location.) It requires a playing stick, two and a half to three and a half feet long and abou an inch in diameter, for each player, and a section of a limb (pref erably of light wood) about five inches long by two and a half to three and a half inches in diameter (or a tin can), which is called the "puck." A shallow hole, large enough to hold the puck easily, is dug in the center of the play area. In a circle around it about twenty fee in diameter small holes are dug an equal distance apart to hold the ends of the sticks of every player minus one.

At a signal, each player runs and places the end of his stick in one of the holes, trying to avoid the larger center one. The player left with the center hole is "It." The players stand behind their sticks. The puck is tossed toward the outter edge of the play area. The purpose of the game is for "It" to knock the puck between the players into the center hole, or to steal one of the outer holes wher no stick is in it. Players in the circle must remove their sticks from the holes to knock the puck out of the ring. Any player may change his position of play by stealing an empty hole in the circle, thereby making the game more interesting and preventing a few players' monopolizing the game by keeping the puck in their area.

If score is kept, each time a player is "It" he has one point against him, and each time he gets the puck in the hole he subtracts two points. Only "It" can put the puck in the center hole. When he does, everyone drops his stick, runs to a designated goal, and returns to get a stick and a hole. The puck is tossed out again to begin a new game. When "It" is able to steal a hole in the circle, every player must return to a hole, to determine who is left out and is therefore the new "It." The play continues with the puck wherever it is.

Can Cricket. Two cans, a softball, and a softball bat are used. Two cans are placed on the ground approximately sixty feet apart. The *pitcher* stands by one can and the *batter* in front of the other, placed in front of the *catcher.* The *runner* stands by the can near the pitcher. The other players are *fielders* and scatter around the playing area. The pitcher rolls the ball in an attempt to knock the can over and the batter attempts to hit the ball croquet style. If the ball is hit, the batter runs to the other can, and at the same time, the runner stationed at the other can runs to the batter's can. They continue to run back and forth as long as they are able to without being put out. The batter and the runner will get one point for each base they reach. The batter is out when a fly ball is caught or when a fielder knocks the can over with the ball before the batter or runner reaches it. The batter continues to run until he is put out. If the can is knocked over, the batter is out. When he is out, the runner moves to the batting position, the catcher to the running position, the pitcher to the catcher's position, and a fielder takes the pitcher's place. The batter moves out to the field.

Do-It-Yourself with Innertubes, Boxes, Plastic Bottles, Rope, and Sticks.

Put any of the above items out, stand back, and watch many games unfold. These items are especially good for free-time play periods.

Idea Starters

Box Fun

Stack them	Hide in them	Toss Items into them
Paint them	Make Villages	Targets
		Obstacle Course

Rope Fun

Jump rope (singles, doubles, group)
Tug-of-War
Knot rope for climbing
Make swings
Make-shift nets
Ground markers

Stick Fun

Use for horses
Bat games
Stick in the Hole
Markers
Relays
Physical feats
Tug-of-War
Balance on hand
Lumi sticks

Innertube Fun

Kick ball
Roll for Distance, Speed, Accuracy
Kick for Distance, Speed, Accuracy
Throw for Distance, Speed, Accuracy
Ring Toss
Relay races around feet
Relay races over body
Hand and throw objects through them

Plastic Bottles

Kick them
Throw them
Bottle baseball
Field markers
Swimming pool fun
Decorations
Obstacle courses for trikes, wagons, bikes

✳

CHAPTER XII

Party Poke
and Its Use

A recreation leader, whether he is experienced or inexperienced, will find it to his advantage to start collecting various items for his Party Poke. Just what is a Party Poke? Simply, it is a collection of various props that the leader might use in presenting a recreational program. As you collect your items, you may want to put them in a small suitcase, a canvas ditty bag, a paper poke (bag), a plain cardboard box, or anything that will be easy to store in a convenient place. This kit should be especially handy when you are called on unexpectedly to lead recreation for a few minutes or for an entire evening's program. As you compile your odds and ends, you may want to prepare a card file listing the items and their uses, i.e.—

Feathers

1. Blowing
   A. Individuals—see who can keep his feather in the air the longest.
   B. Groups—which group can keep it in the air.
      Relay—blow along floor or in air to a goal line.
      Blanket football—four teams, one on each side, holding blanket shoulder high, try to blow feather off other team's side.

Here are some suggested items for your Poke:

Alphabet Cards (see end of chapter)

Balloons

Relay—As each person gets to the head of the line, he must blow up his balloon, go to a chair and sit on the balloon until it pops, then return to the foot of the line.
Sword fight—A thumb tack is scotch-taped to the tip of a long "air

ship" balloon which has been inflated, then each person "sword fights" with his balloon, trying to pop the balloons of others while protecting his own.

Balloon Basketball

Balloon Soccer

Beans (dried)

Bean Art—One person drops a small handful of beans on a stack of small sheets of paper, then uses a hat pin to punch holes at the position of the beans on the paper. Each person is given one of these pieces of paper and a pencil and is to connect the pin punctures to form whatever picture he can visualize from them.

Yes and No—Give each person ten beans. If you catch someone saying "yes" or "no," they give you a bean. The one who ends up with the most beans wins.

Bottle Caps

Use for tossing games, Indian Corn, dropping into bottles, checkers, etc.

Chalk

Blackboard Art—Start with letters or numbers, and have each person add something to form a picture.

Use to draw dividing lines, goal lines, four-square ball court, etc., in relays and other games.

Dice

Play "Kootie"

Droodles

Draw droodles on large sheets of paper and have groups guess what the droodles represent. Good for a party starter.

Feathers

Jar Rings

Use for ring toss; place rings on floor and toss bottle caps or buttons into them, etc.

Newspapers

Newspaper costumes—groups fashion costume for one member from newspaper.

Newspaper Swat—roll up newspapers and use for different types of swatting games.

Pencil and Paper

These will be the most versatile pieces of equipment in your kit. Almost every recreation book has a section on pencil and paper games.

Paper Plates

Use for tossing games—throwing through a wire hoop or into a waste paper basket. Use to make funny faces, for making hats.

Paper Bags

Nose Bag Drama—put various items in paper bag. Give one bag to each group, and have them work out a skit using the items in their bag.

Paper Bag Puppets

Ping Pong Balls

Table Football—On a ping pong or rectangular table, have two teams, one on each side of the table. The object is to blow ping pong ball off other team's side.

Bounce and catch in paper cups.

Rubber Bands

Funny Face—Have each person pull rubber band over his head, down to the neck, and then up in front to rest on the tip of the nose. The object then is to work the band back down the neck, using only face movements, no hands or shoulders.

Socks

Bean bags—fill with beans and use for bean bags.

Fill with objects to be identified by feeling.

Soda Straws

Straw Relay—Have first person of each team hold a piece of paper on end of straw by inhaling. The object is to see which team can pass it to the end of the line from straw to straw.

Straw and Feather Relay—Blow through a straw to move a feather which has been placed on the floor to a designated goal.

String

String over body—Make a loop of string large enough to pass over the largest person in group. Give each team a loop and have each person on team pass the loop over his body. The team to finish first wins.
Ring on a String
String Handcuffs
Use for nets and boundary markers.

Toothpicks

Toothpick tower—Build a triangle tower on mouth of a milk bottle, having each person add one toothpick, and continue until tower topples.
Toothpick-Paper Clip Relay—Each person in line has a toothpick in his mouth. First person of each team is given a paper clip, which he passes by toothpick to the next person, and so on to the end of the line.

Wit

Collection of stunts, skits, stories, songs.
Creative Session—Place Poke on table. Give participants the opportunity to make up their own games and party from what they find in the Poke.
Caution . . . Develop a method of getting your equipment returned. It will be scattered all over the place if you don't.
You will want to have a few items such as scissors, scotch tape, staple gun, crayons, thumb tacks, glue, etc.

These are just a few suggestions and should not be considered as complete in supplying your Party Poke. By all means, create a Party Poke that fits your needs. You will have a lot of fun creating new games and will come to the realization that, with a handful of props and some imagination, you can lead others into a rich experience in recreation.

Points:

1 - Body
2 - Head
3 - Eyes
4 - Feelers
5 - Tail
6 - Legs

Kootie

Directions:
The game is played by four persons using one die. The player across from you becomes your partner for that game. The die is thrown until a one appears; the partners then each draw a body and the one rolling rolls again. If he gets a two, the head is drawn, and he continues to roll, trying to roll all six numbers in order, until he can't add anything to the Kootie. If not, the throw passes to the next player clockwise. A complete Kootie is drawn here for an example and is worth a total of 78 points. The first team to finish yells "Kootie," and then all players total their scores and change partners for a new game. Player with highest total score wins.

Fun With Alphabet Cards

An entire evening of fun can be planned with the use of alphabet cards. A few suggestions follow. Ask a committee to create their own activities.

Alphabet Race. Two tables are placed at one end of the room. Each must be large enough to hold a complete alphabet, each letter on a separate card or paper plate. The alphabets should be scrambled and spread out enough so that all letters may be seen. A different colored alphabet should be used for each team. Divide the group into two teams which stand at opposite ends of the room, each in a line facing the tables. The leader tells a story. Whenever he finishes a sentence, players from each team run up to the table and find the letters necessary to spell the last word in the sentence. For instance, if the sentence ended with the word "crime," the first five players in each line run up, find the letters, turn and face their own team in the order that spells the word correctly. The team that spells the word first wins a point. The players then return their letters to the tables and go to the back of their respective lines. The leader then continues the story. Of course, no words containing the same letter twice should end a sentence. An impartial judge stands back with the team.

Flash Cards. The leader needs one set of cards. The letters should be large enough to be seen by all. Here are some uses: (1) Tell a story and hold up a letter. The first person who names the object called for (name of an automobile beginning with that letter, or a proper name, name of a city or of a famous person, famous product, etc.) gets the letter to hold for counting points. (2) Grocery Store. Divide group into two teams. When a letter is held up, the first side mentioning an item in a grocery store which begins with that letter gets a point for his side. (3) Use the idea with other type stores, Biblical characters, things you would see on a nature hike, musical terms, things you would see in a garage, etc.

Punch Words. Pin a letter of the alphabet on everyone—duplicating a few vowels. Give everyone a 3 x 5 card. At the signal to start, each person attempts to find three others whose letters plus his own will form a four letter word. The group then appears before a judge who punches each one's card. The individuals then find others and form new four letter words. Speed is essential. The winner is the person with the most punches in his card. The game is best played when there are several judges and a definite time limit.

Just-One-Word. The eleven letters of the words "just-one-word" are distributed to players of each team, and they are told to get together in such an order as to spell "just-one-word." The uninitiated will probably try to spell one word, instead of the catch. Be rather certain that no one of the group knows the answer ahead of time.

Scrambles. Participants seated around room—no particular order. Prepare a list of questions with single word answers. The leader scrambles the answer word by thumbtacking the individual letters to a board in front of the audience. The question to which the scrambled letters are the answer is then asked. The section of the audience first responding with the answer receives a point.

Alphabet Charades. Two parallel lines face each other. Each player has an alphabet card. The first player in one of the lines shows his card and goes down to the end of the line acting out an adjective which starts with his letter. If the player can get back to position without the other team guessing the adjective being acted, the player stays with his team. If the other side is successful in guessing, the player changes teams. This is repeated alternately until each has performed.

✳

CHAPTER XIII

Fun with Informal Dramatics, Stories, and Puppets

The field of dramatics lends itself to numerous recreational activities. Among these are dramatic type games, situation dramas, story telling, and dramatization, paper bag drama, charades, shadow drama, dramatization of songs and poems ("Shooting of Dan McGrew," nursery rhymes, "Hiawatha"), skits, stunts, pantomime, puppetry, and others. Younger elementary-age children particularly enjoy dramatic games. Junior high age young people enjoy dramatic games which stimulate the mental processes. Many of these games may be used by the drama director to put a new group at ease.

Situation Drama. This type of drama can be done effectively by dividing the guests into three or four small groups (there are those who suggest no more than ten people to a group but larger groups are effective if the leader generates sufficient enthusiasm and adapts for the situation). Each group creates its own story, characterizations, and production, including properties, costumes, and sets. Often the people themselves portray inanimate objects—a swinging door, a water cooler, a slot machine, typewriters, showers, automobiles, and so on. In informal dramatics, properties consist of whatever there is to be found at hand. For instance, a ping-pong paddle for a tongue depresser, a coat hanger for the horns of a bull, a large strainer for a catcher's mask for baseball, a lamp shade for a hat, and whatever else the imagination produces. The average person is apt to be freer in improvised dramatics than he is in the more formal drama with a script in his hand. He is apt to have a more creative experience because he understands the material which he has helped to create and in which he can choose his own characterization, whether it be human, animal, or inanimate.

The leader explains the activity, provides a situation which is the same for all groups, and then each unit goes off for 15-20 mintues, or whatever time is needed, to work on its presentation. Each skit is acted out before the other groups. Each group should feel free to incorporate pantomime, dialogue, narration, or a combination of any of these.

Possible situations are as follows:

1. A group of people somewhere are engaged in some activity. Someone comes in and robs them of something. What does the group do about it? (This provides the opportunity for a three-act skit.)

2. A cold night in Moscow.

3. Each group creates a situation that must end with the words, "Oh, my goodness, it's twelve o'clock!"

4. The group finds a wallet.

It is not difficult to work up some interesting situations or adaptations of your own. One church group varied this type of drama by giving each group a slip of paper with the name of some spot on earth. Skits were developed to show how they returned from that spot to the location of the party. Possibilities are the Great Wall of China, the top of an Egyptian pyramid, etc.

Paper Bag Drama. Prepare in advance a number of paper bags containing various odds and ends to stir the imagination. There should be the same number of paper bags as number of groups participating. Each paper bag should contain the same properties. Use whatever happens to be handy—a magazine, piece of string, crepe paper, gum wrappers, pecan, flower, pine cone, tooth pick, vegetables, fruit, marshmallow, pencil and pen, etc.

Divide the guests into a number of groups. Provide a paper bag full of properties for each group and give them a time limit to create a skit based on and using the materials in the bag. Groups take turns presenting their skits to the other groups.

Paper Bag Puppets. A paper bag may be made into a puppet by turning it upside down and slipping a hand into the opening of the bag and working the fingers into the fold at the bottom of the bag. When the fingers are moved up and down the effect is that of a mouth opening and closing.

In the particular situation being described, a young adult church school class scheduled a family party. Following a "pot luck" dinner, the smaller children were taken to a nursery in another part of the church. Four tables were supplied with a great many odds and ends of materials—paper bags, cotton, rubber bands, napkins, crepe paper, scissors, crayons, glue, wall paper, yarn, and any other articles which might be used in the construction of a paper bag puppet. The families were divided and grouped around the tables, three or four families to a table. Each group was asked to select a nursery story, work out the characters with the materials at hand, and rehearse for the show to follow. The participants set about cutting out ears, coloring a facial design, gluing on yarn for hair, adding cotton for cheeks, and so on. One man used his cigarette lighter to melt different colored crayons to color the cotton head of the Big Bad Wolf he had created.

A puppet stage had been set up in another room. After the rehearsal of the skits, the nursery children were brought in and the groups took turns presenting their skits. The evening was closed with a period of singing.

This activity may also be readily adapted and introduced to other groups.

Charades. The guests are divided into two teams and are seated in line facing each other. One team selects a descriptive word, phrase, or sentence. This is whispered to the representative of the other team. The representative must return to his team and, by the use of pre-arranged signals and pantomime, attempt to communicate to his team the word or phrase. If he is successful, his team is awarded a point. If he fails within a time limit, the first team receives a point. Points may be subtracted for wrong guesses.

If props are used, have on hand a supply of old hats, scarves, pieces of string, cardboard, newspapers, crayons, and any other objects which might possibly be used with the words or phrases which have been planned.

Such words as the following may be acted out (act each syllable separately, then the whole word):

Accidental: Axe . . . sigh . . . dent . . . tall
Automobile: Ought . . toe . . . mow . . . bill
Cantelope: Can't . . . elope
Dogmatic: Dog . . . mat . . . tick
Handkerchief: Hand . . . cur . . . chief
Hurricane: Hurry . . . cane, or Her . . . eye . . . cane
Infancy: Inn . . . fan . . . see
Impudent: Imp . . . pew . . . dent
Jealousy: Jell . . . us . . . see
Moccasin: Mock . . . cuss . . . sin

Presbyterian: Press . . . by . . . teary . . . Ann
Robinson Crusoe: Rob . . . inn . . . son . . . crew . . . sew
Situation: Sit . . . chew . . . weigh (or way) . . . shun
Superflous: Soup . . . purr . . . flew . . . us

Dramatic Poem. The following poem is read or recited. Group response is made to each motion: Thumb up—"Hurrah;" Thumb down—"Boo"; Sweeping motion of hand—"Ahhh"; Pushing palm of hand outward—"Shhhh."

In the days of old when knights were bold (up)
And barons held their sway (around)
A warrior bold with spurs of gold (down)
Sang merrily his lay (up)
Sang merrily his lay (down)
My love is young and fair (round)
My love hath golden hair (out)
And eyes so blue and heart so true (down)
That none with her compare (round)
So what care I though death be nigh (round)
I'll live for love or die (down)
So what care I though death be nigh (up)
I'll live for love or die (out)
So this brave knight in armour bright (round)
Went gaily to the fight (out)
And fought the fight but during the night (out)
His soul had passed away (up)
His soul had passed away (down)
The plighted ring he wore was crushed and wet with gore (round)
Yet ere he died he bravely cried (up)
I have kept the vow I swore (down)
So what care I though death be nigh (round)
I've fought for love and died (up)
For love (up), for love (up), I die (down)

Winter Adventure.

Sounds: Wind—Who-o-o
Grandfather clock—Tick-tock noises with tongue
Asleep—Snore noises
Cow—Moo-ooo

Rain—Hands gently slapping on knees
Cat—Purr or wild meo-o-o-ow
Part of the group are assigned to each noise. Rain and grandfather clock can be doubled with one of the other noises. Rain and wind go on for most of the time, the grandfather clock through the whole sketch.

The farmhouse was silent except for the ticking of the grandfather clock (ticking sound). All the folk were asleep (snore). Soon the rain and wind began to blow (blowing sound) gently at first, then harder and harder (wind blows harder). Still the folk slept (snores) until there was tremendous noise out at the barn (bang!!).

The cow began to call (moo) excitedly, and soon it sounded as if there were trouble in the barnyard. The famer sprang to his feet, rushed out to the barn. The cow was mooing excitedly (moo). He saw the barn door open and banging. When he examined the cow, he saw the reason for her mooing (moo). She had fallen down and strained her milk!

So he gave her some hay and fixed the door. The wind was still blowing (blowing sound). He drew his coat around him and ran for the house. Inside, he drew up to the nice warm fire and took his chair. The cat purred (purr) by his chair, and gradually, without intending to, the farmer went to sleep again (snore). Gradually the rain became lighter (lighter rain), and the wind died down (softer wind), and after a while it was calm. All that could be heard in the farmhouse were the soft purr of the cat (purr) and the gentle snore of the farmer (snore) and the quiet ticking of the old grandfather clock (tick-tock).

Stage. Group divided into seven sections. Each small group responds with activity when his characterization is mentioned in the story.

1. cowboys	Driving stage--"head'em up, move'em out"
2. Indians	War dance and yell
3. women	Scream
4. horses	Trot, beating tatto on floor, etc.
5. stagecoach	Stand, turn around, sit
6. rifles	Stand, aim and fire "Bang!"
7. bows and arrows	Stand, draw bow and "Twang!"

It was in the day of STAGECOACHES, and COWBOYS, and INDIANS. Alkali Ike, Dippy Dick, and Pony Pete were three courageous COWBOYS. When the STAGECOACH left for Rainbow's End they were aboard, as were also two WOMEN, Salty Sal and a doll-faced blonde. The STAGECOACH was drawn by three handsome HORSES and it left Dead End exactly on time.

The most dangerous part of the journey was the pass known as Gory Gulch. As the STAGECOACH neared this spot it could be noticed that the WOMEN were a bit nervous and the COWBOYS were alert, fingering their RIFLES as if to be ready for any emergency. Even the HORSES seemed to sense danger.

Sure enough, just as the STAGECOACH entered the Gulch, there sounded the blood-curdling war cry of the INDIANS. Mounted on HORSES they came riding wildly toward the STAGECOACH, aiming their BOWS AND ARROWS. The COWBOYS took aim with their RIFLES and fired. The WOMEN screamed. The HORSES pranced nervously. The INDIANS shot their BOWS AND ARROWS. The COWBOYS aimed their RIFLES again, this time shooting with more deadly effect. The leading brave fell and the INDIANS turned their HORSES and fled leaving their BOWS AND ARROWS behind. The WOMEN fainted. The COWBOYS shot one more volley from their RIFLES, just for luck. The driver urged on the HORSES and the STAGECOACH sped down the trail.

Moustache Special. Select several players from the group to participate in this stunt. Ask them to sit in a row of chairs facing the audience. Provide each one with a two-inch piece of electrician's plastic tape which he applies over his upper lip. Each person tries to loosen the tape by using only facial muscles. Play music at different tempos to increase the interest.

Flying Illusion. An inexpensive mirror about 1 foot by 4 feet in length (the kind that can be purchased in dime stores) and a hat are needed for this stunt. The leader has an assistant. The guests are brought one at a time into the room where the stunt is being performed. The mirror is placed lengthwise along the top edge of a table, which should be a little shorter than the mirror, with the mirror facing outward from the table. A box is placed behind the mirror to support it and prevent the guests from looking behind it. A chair is placed at one end of the mirror facing toward it. The first guest arrives and the assistant seats him in the chair, asks him to place his cheek against the end of the mirror (about midway between top and bottom on the mirror side) facing the leader at the other end of the mirror. The leader is standing, bent over, with his hat on his head and his nose pressed against the end of the mirror so that the guest sees half of his face outside the mirror and the other half in the mirror—it looks like one entire head. The leader has his hand on the rim of the hat on the back side of the mirror where the guest cannot see it. He asks the guest to blow gently in his direction and, as the guest does so, moves the hat gently up off his head and back onto it again—the guest has the illusion of the hat rising by itself! After doing this a couple of times, the leader asks the guest to blow hard, and the hat immediately disappears to the rear of the mirror as the leader gives it a yank—a mystifying illusion! The guest is asked to blow again with extra concentration and effort, and the leader raises his leg and arm, the ones which the guest can actually see, perpendicular to the mirror. The mirror reveals another leg and arm being raised (reflection), and then guest sees the illusion of the leader being suspended in space! Many guests will be completely baffled! Ask the guest to remain and watch the others as they participate in the stunt.

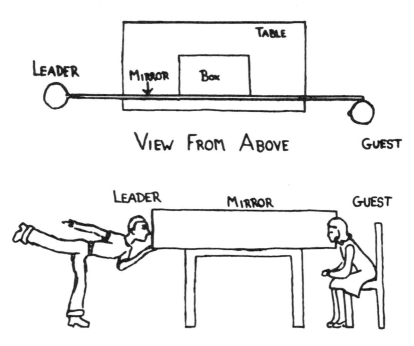

Handkerchief Puppetry

The stories below may be used while folding handkerchief puppets, which are shown on the following pages.

The Rabbit

Ren had a pet rabbit and one day he checked the cage and the rabbit was gone! Ren went looking for his rabbit. At the edge of the field he saw a big tree, and sticking out on one side of the tree he saw a little white ear. As he got closer to the tree he noticed another white ear, and just as he got to the tree—out hopped his pet rabbit!

The Mouse

Beth lived in a house that had a downstairs and an upstairs. One day she heard a noise that sounded like a mouse, so she looked through the house—downstairs and upstairs. She even went into the attic, but she couldn't find the mouse! She decided to pack a picnic lunch in her basket and go to the country. When it was time to eat, she looked in her basket and there was nothing in it! Then she heard a noise! She shook the basket upside down and out jumped a little mouse. They became very good friends, and everywhere that Beth went, she took the little mouse along.

Handkerchief Puppet

Once upon a time there was a handkerchief puppet, Lee Ann, who had a terrible temper. The sad part about it was that each time she lost her temper, she lost her head! It wasn't until someone spoke the magic word that she would find her head again. When she found her head, she was very happy until the next time she lost her temper.

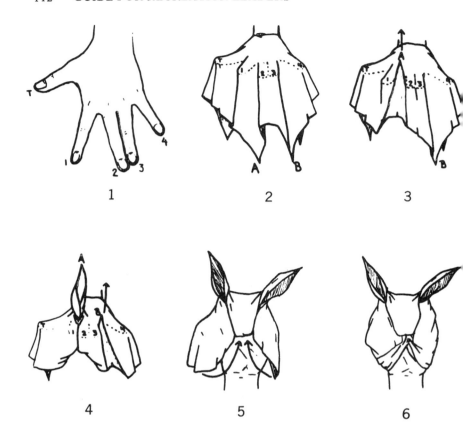

1   2   3

4   5   6

TO MAKE A RABBIT:

1. Hold hand as shown with second and third fingers together.
2. Hold hand in horizontal position with palm down. Drape handkerchief over hand as shown so that corners A and B hang evenly.
3. Place corner A between first and second fingers. Close fingers one and two and pull A up to form rabbit's ear.
4. Place corner B between third and fourth fingers. Close fingers three and four and pull B up to form rabbit's ear.
5. Tuck the remaining cloth up under the fingers. Press thumb against first finger to hold cloth.
6. The finished rabbit should resemble the above drawing.

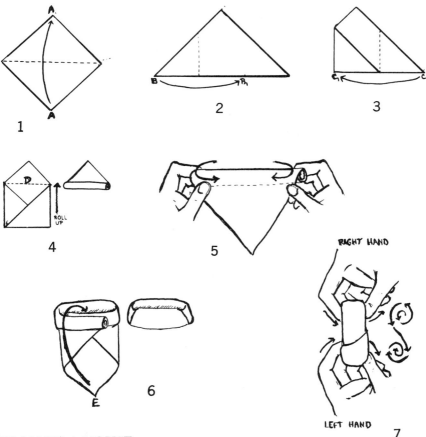

TO MAKE A MOUSE:

1. Fold corner A to opposite corner A^1 to form a triangle.
2. Fold corner B to B^1.
3. Fold corner C to C^1.
4. Starting at the bottom roll up tightly to line D.
5. Hold as illustrated so that roll is facing away from you. Fold ends towards yourself so that they overlap 1½ inches.
6. Bring corner E up towards yourself and over overlapping ends and tuck in tightly.
7. Using 1st and 2nd fingers of left hand continue to tuck in and begin to roll tightly. At the same time unroll the other side with the right hand. The result should be a continuous rolling (left hand) and unrolling (right hand) motion.

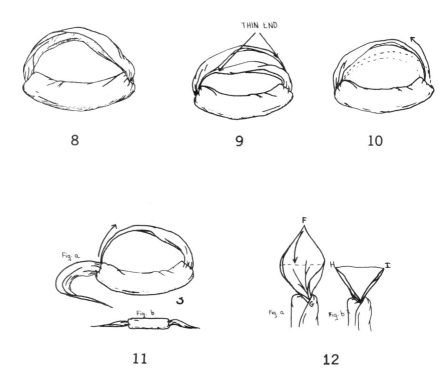

8. Continue this process (rolling very tightly) until there is a break in the fabric and a basket (above) is formed.
9. Separate the handle into two sections. Note that each section has one end which is thinner than the other.
10. Take hold of the thin end which is to your right. While holding everything else very firmly so that it will not come apart pull the thin end out and over to your left.
11. Take hold of the thin end to your left. While holding everything else very firmly so that it will not come apart pull the thin end out and over to your right. It should now look like Fig. b.
12. Take one of the ends you have just pulled out and spread it out as flat as possible. Fold corner F down to G so that it looks like Fig. b.

13. To make the mouse's head tie an overhand knot using the two ends H and I.
14. The finished mouse should resemble the above drawing.
15. Hold mouse in palm of left hand so that the tail rests against the fingers. Stroke mouse with right hand.
16. At the end of each stroke the right hand should cover the fingers of the left hand and the rear section of the mouse.
17. Holding the right hand so that it hides the left, use the fingers of the left hand to shoot the mouse out thus making it appear to jump out of your hands.

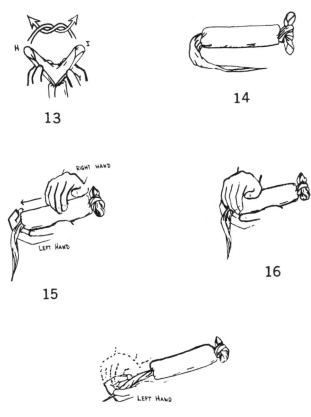

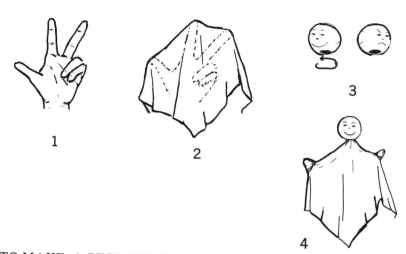

TO MAKE A PING PONG BALL PUPPET:

1. Hold hand as shown.
2. Drape handkerchief or piece of cloth over hand.
3. Cut hole in ping pong ball large enough for index finger. A different face can be drawn on each side of the ball.
4. Place ping pong ball on index finger and tie rubber bands around thumb and second finger.

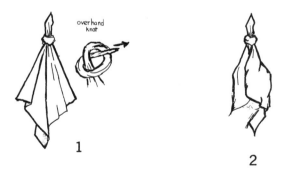

TO MAKE AN INDIAN:

1. At one corner of the handkerchief tie an overhand knot pulling end through an inch to an inch and a half.
2. Insert index finger into knot. Wrap handkerchief around hand and hold closed with fingers.

CHAPTER XIV
Fun for the Handicapped

Following are some principles to have in mind when planning and implementing recreational events with the handicapped:

1. Handicapped persons have as much right to a variety of recreational and camping activities as do the non-handicapped.

2. Look around the community to discover where the handicapped are, make contact, make plans, plan and implement recreational activities.

3. The physically and mentally handicapped are not recreationally handicapped.

4. The handicapped have the same hopes, the same fears, and the same ambitions as the non-handicapped.

5. Focus on the person—not the handicap.

6. Plans for recreation should be make in light of the following goals:

Personal fulfillment
Democratic human relations
Development of leisure skills and interests
Health and fitness
Creative expression
Aesthetic appreciation

7. Participants are best motivated if they can "voluntarily" select their activities. For example, they may be given a chance to initiate programs.

8. Emphasize what handicapped persons can do; don't worry about what they can't do. For example, many (or even "most") physically handicapped are mentally alert. This suggests the possibility of mentally stimulating games and activities.

9. Leaders must be patient, persistent, and positive-thinking.

10. Encourage interaction and closer interpersonal relationships with other persons, handicapped and non-handicapped.

11. Provide a non-threatening (no physical barriers), non-demanding (no climbing stairs) environment.

12. Help develop feeling of self-acceptance and importance.

13. Encourage socially acceptable behavior.

14. Enrich attitudes, interests, and experiences.

15. Encourage creative, inventive, and expressive efforts.

16. Leader should "be himself" when working with the handicapped.

17. Remember that the person with a handicap is a person! He is like anyone else, except for the special limitations of his handicap.

18. Talk about the same things as you would with anyone else.

19. Help handicapped persons only when they request it.

20. Leader should not make up his mind ahead of time about handicapped persons. He may be surprised at how wrong he is in judging their interests and abilities.

21. Orient the participants outward toward community life.

22. Even though working with a large group, try to make the experience personal for everyone.

Activities

There is a wide range of activities for all handicapped persons in books, pamphlets, and articles which can be of great assistance to a leader. Many of these activities require an impressive array of expensive indoor and outdoor equipment and supplies. Let us instead think instead simply, and consider programming which requires no equipment or supplies. For example:

Use of the voice: Activities which may be conducted are: singing, choral speaking, chanting, poetry, imitation, dramatic play, whispering play, storytelling, conversation, debating teams, etc.

Use of the body: Activities which may be conducted are: all types of exercises such as Yoga, isometric, aerobics, calisthentics, dance forms of every kind, marching, stretching, rolling, crawling, etc.

Use of hands and arms: Activities which may be conducted singly or in combination are: clapping, shaking, grasping, touching, slapping, tapping, feeling, opening and closing fists, finger play, lifting, raising, striking, etc.

Use of feet and legs: Activities which may be conducted to possibly lead into games and relays are: stamping, swinging, hopping, jumping, bending, etc.

Use of silence: Activities which may be conducted in silence are: pantomime, dancing, making faces, Yoga postures, deep breathing, rest with eyes closed, meditating, thinking, word images, looking, smelling, tasting, listening, touching, etc.

More activities are possible when you have at least an equal number of non-handicapped as handicapped participating together. Here are a few guidelines and suggestions of activities that are possible for fun with the handicapped.

1. Select activities that may be slowed to whatever pace needed for full participation.

2. Don't expect everyone to be able to do exactly the same thing, i.e., some activities might exclude a few but are good for those who can take part.

3. Pair up non-handicapped with handicapped when conducting activities requiring partners.

4. When grouping for activities, determine beforehand if it is best to have all of one type of handicapped together or if it is best to mix the group.

The following activities have been used with a high degree of success.

Settings: A crippled children's hospital—variety of handicapped.

Room Arrangement: Large room with participants arranged in a large circle facing the center of the circle. Participants are in wheel chairs, on litters, crib beds, three-wheel carts, chairs, etc.

Leadership: All non-handicapped facing one of the handicapped.

Activity: "Alley Cat" . . . a dance usually done with the feet as follows:

> Touch right toe out to the right, return to place
> Repeat
> Touch left toe out to the left, return to place
> Repeat
> Touch right toe to the back, return to place
> Repeat
> Touch left toe to the back, return to place
> Repeat
> Lift right knee across left leg, return to place
> Repeat
> Lift left knee across right leg, return to place
> Repeat

Lift right knee across left leg, return to place
Lift left knee across right leg, return to place
Clap own hands
Jump ¼ turn to your own right
Now to adapt: Have everyone move any part of the body two times in a row for each time the dance requires a movement, i.e., instead of reaching out with the right foot, reach out with the right hand or nod the head to the right twice. In place of the jump, everyone yells out "Hey!"

Activity: Use of Imagination Games:

Balloon Fun

Give everyone an imaginary balloon (Caution: the leader must be sold on doing this type of game. At times they are a lot more fun than using traditional type activities.)
Start soft background music

1. Blow the balloon into the air and watch it float down.
2. Tap the balloon with whatever part of the body you want to and keep it up in the air. (A girl was observed in a body cast keeping her balloon up with only her toes.)
3. Bat your balloon to someone else. When the music stops, hold your balloon. When the music starts, bat it to someone else and keep the batting going.

Musical Movement

1. Dance a part of your body as if you were a feather!
2. Dance a part of your body as if you were a lead ball!
3. Dance a part of your body as if you were a chicken!
4. Dance a part of your body as if you were a fish!

Square Dancing can be fun if a few guidelines are followed:

Use forward movements more than circle movements.
Use bows and nods rather than swings.
Keep movements in straight lines.
Keep hands joined down, especially for those who use hand walkers, etc.
Pair up non-handicapped with handicapped.

Calls for a Big Circle Square Dance

All join hands and go forward and back (or all bow to the middle)

Bow to your partner, bow to your corner

Two couples face each other (one facing counter-clockwise around the circle and the other clockwise)

Bow to the opposite

Go foreward and back

The most able couple go forward and around that couple and take a little peek

Back to the center and bow to your partner

Go around that couple and peek once more

Back to the center and everybody bow to your partner

All pass to a new couple and repeat the dances called from "Bow to the opposite"

(When passing to a new couple, follow the rule of the road and all pass forward to their own right.)

Consult any good square dance books for other figures that might be adapted.

Most of all, believe that it can be done!

Resources

Recreation Equipment for the Disabled. Available free from North American Recreation Convertibles, Inc., Bridgeport, Conn. 06601

Fun is Therapeutic, Ardis Stevens. Springfield, Ill.: Charles C. Thomas. Contains suggestions to assist the leader of recreation with the ill and handicapped and directions for a variety of activities.

The Physically Handicapped and the Community, Louis A. Michaux. Springfield, Ill.: Charles C. Thomas. Contains suggestions about the role of church and community in working with the handicapped.

Recreation Center for the Handicapped, Inc., Great Highway, San Francisco, California. Write for bibliography of resources which are available free or at minimal expense.

Specifications for Making Buildings and Facilities Accessible To *and Usable by the Physically Handicapped.* Available from America National Standards Institute, Inc., 1430 Broadway, New York, N.Y 10018.

Recreation for the Handicapped, A Selection of Recent Book and Pamphlets. Available from The National Easter Seal Society fo Crippled Children and Adults, 2023 W. Ogden Ave., Chicago, Illinoi 60612.

Handi-Quipment Games, Ardis Stevens. Brattleboro Retreat Brattleboro, Vermont. Helps and directions for playing recreatior equipment games with the handicapped.

When You Meet a Handicapped Person. Fifteen hints for reward ing relationships. Available from National Easter Seal Society.

"Toys, Games and Apparatus for Children with Cerebral Palsy." Available from National Easter Seal Society.

Aids and Appliances. Helps for working with the blind. Available from American Foundation for the Blind, 16 West 16th Street, New York, N.Y. 10011.

Games for Recreation and Rehabilitation. Free leaflet available from World Wide Games, Inc., Box 450, Deleware, Ohio 43015.

*

CHAPTER XV

Fun Songs

There are numerous fun songs (stunt songs, motion songs) which may be used effectively for events with children (camp programs, parties, summer playground, etc.) and family programs. Many are suitable for youth and adults if the mood of the group lends itself to this type of activity.

Fun songs are probably used best in getting a group started or to quiet it down toward the end of a program.

Following are several, some adapted to familiar tunes and some which will be new:

Row, Row, Row Your Boat

Sing first as a round. Then have everyone sing together—standing on the first line, sitting on the second line, standing on the third line, and sitting on the last line. Repeat again as a round with groups standing and sitting at appropriate times. Sing through the song two or three times.

Shortnin' Bread

Another "gimmick." Sing the chorus first as usual. Ask the group to repeat and leave out the word "shortnin'." Fun! Usually too much "bread"! Add the verses, still leaving out the word "shortnin'."

Head and Shoulders

(Tune: "Tavern in the Town")
Point to the parts of body indicated by words. Repeat and sing faster.

Head and shoulders, knees and toes, knees and toes
Head and shoulders, knees and toes, knees and toes
Eyes and ears and mouth and nose
Head and shoulders, knees and toes, knees and toes.

The More We Get Together

On words "friend" and "together," stand if seated and sit if standing.

The more we get together, together, together,
The more we get together
The happier we'll be.
For your friends are my friends
And my friends are your friends.
The more we get together the happier we'll be.

I Had A Little Pig

(Sing up the scale, one note for each line—come down the scale with the "oinks"—stand and shout "Pork Chops!")

I had a little pig
He had a curly tail
He grew so very fat
That I took him to a sale
And now that he is gone
I'm feeling quite forsaken
I sold him to the butcher
And now he's breakfast bacon
Oink, oink, oink, oink, oink, oink, oink, oink
Pork chops!

(Group may stand and sit slowly as they sing up and down the scale.)

Funiculi, Funicula

The participants do not have to know the words. Ask them to "da-da-da" the tune once to make sure they are familiar with it. Divide the participants into three groups. The first group sings "ho" when the leader points to it, the second group sings "he" when the leader points to it, and the third group sings "ha." The first group begins singing and, as the song progresses, the leader points from one to another and they respond by singing and repeating their syllable with the tune.

ush the Damper In

(Excellent with small children)

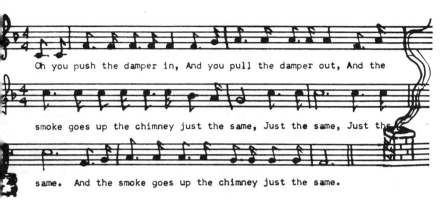

Oh you push the damper in, And you pull the damper out, And the

smoke goes up the chimney just the same, Just the same, Just the

same. And the smoke goes up the chimney just the same.

Each time the song is repeated, leave out the next complete hrase, and use only the motions.

"Oh you push the damper in"—pretend to grasp a handle with the fist and push it away from the body

"And you pull the damper out"—pull back toward body

"And the smoke goes up the chimney just the same"—spiral motion with hands into the air

"Just the same"—swing one hand to the side

"Just the same"—swing the other hand to the other side

"And the smoke goes up the chimney just the same"—spiral motion

Minnihaha

(Good camp song)

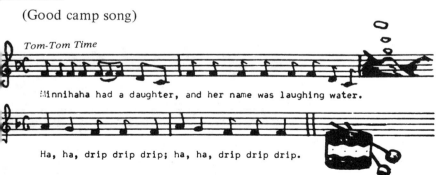

Tom-Tom Time

Minnihaha had a daughter, and her name was laughing water.

Ha, ha, drip drip drip; ha, ha, drip drip drip.

Sing through once. Add the chant "Same song, second verse" an repeat song. Keep repeating until ready for the last verse and chan "Same song, last verse, sing it louder, make it worse." Sing one mor time.

One of My Thumbs

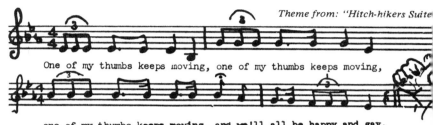

Theme from: "Hitch-hikers Suite"

One of my thumbs keeps moving, one of my thumbs keeps moving, one of my thumbs keeps moving, and we'll all be happy and gay.

Hold up one fist and wiggle thumb while singing the first verse On the second verse sing "Two of my thumbs keep moving" an wiggle two thumbs.
On the third verse sing "Two of my thumbs, one arm, kee moving" and begin rotating one arm in addition to wiggling two thumbs.
Fourth verse: Two of my thumbs, two arms, etc.
Fifth verse: Two of my thumbs, two arms, one leg, etc.
Sixth verse: Two of my thumbs, two arms, two legs, etc.
Seventh verse: Two of my thumbs, two arms, two legs, stand up turn around, sit down, etc.

Ham and Eggs

(Good camp song)

"Fast Fare"

Ham and eggs, ham and eggs; I like mine fried good and brown, I like mine fried upside down. Ham and eggs, ham and eggs; Flip 'em, flop 'em, flip 'em, flop 'em, ham and eggs.

Sing once as is and then sing the words in reverse:
Eggs and ham, eggs and ham:
Brown and good fried mine like I,
Down side up fried mine like I.
Eggs and ham, eggs and ham;
'em flip, 'em flop, 'em flip, 'em flop, eggs and ham.

1y Dame Had a Lame Tame Crane

(Tricky round, appropriate for youth and adults)

My dame had a lame tame crane. My dame had a crane that was lame. Oh

pray gentle Jane, let my dame's lame tame crane, Drink and come home a-

gain.

Index

Alphabet Cards 102
Animal Exchange 45
Apples, Oranges, Peaches,
Plums 40
Arches 27
Article Exchange 29

Back-to-Back Relay 87
Balloon Fan Relay 86
Balloon Pop Relay 86
Balloons, activities with 53-56
Barnyard 42
Barter 32
Beater Goes Round 90
Block Head Relay 84
Book Baffler 76
Bottle Baseball 91
Bow-Legged Relay 85
Bowling Relay 86
Buzz 49

Can Cricket 95
Carnival Night 58
Cat and Mouse 38
Catch, Throw, and Squat 85
Chair Relays 52
Charades 106
Chicken and Grasshopper 41
Choo Choo Train 31
Circle Relay 51
Clap Alphabet 20
Clap-Pass 20
Closing the Door 90
Come Along 26
Corner Spry 92
Counting Fingers 21
Crab Race 86
Crossed Wires 20
Crooked Walk Relay 87

Ding-a-Lings 78-83
Donkeys, Goats, and
Monkeys 22
Don't Say "Yes" 16
Droodles 17
Duck, Duck, Goose 90

Egg Blowing 16

Face to Face 32
Family Musical Mixer 35

Feelavision 15
Fire on the Mountain 37
Flying Dutchman 37
Flying Illusion 109
Folded Chair Relay 86
Four Square Ball 92
French Cricket 93
Fun Around the Clock 33

Game Mixers 31-34
Ghost 50
Going Camping 41
Going to Minneapolis 74
Guess Who 16

Handkerchief Puppetry 111
Hare Today, Goon
Tomorrow 24
Head and Shoulders 25
Heads or Tails 23
Hello, Ladies 30
Hoop Relay 88
Horse and Rider Relay 87
House of Hands 21
How Do You Like Your
Neighbor? 42

I'm Thinking of a Word 48
In the Manner of the
Adverb 48
Indianapolis Speedway 44
Island Mixer 28

Johnny Says 23

Kick the Can 93
Kootie 101

Lemonade 38
Loose Caboose 31

Magazine Magic 75
Magic Money 76
Malaga Grapes 78
Matching 77
Matching Beans 16
Mathematics 24
Measuring Worm Relay 88
Menagerie 46
Merry Mixup 89
Message Relay 85
Mirrors 21
Money Magic 76
Moon Game 73
Moustache Special 109
Musical Elbows 43
Musical Handshakes 29
Musical Mixers 26-31
My Father Bought a Dog 44

Name Hunt 34
Name Tag Mixer 33
Name Your Neighbor 32
Newspaper Golf 16
Newspaper Relay 88
Nicknames 34
Numbers Mixer 32

Old Plug 9
One-and-All Relay 8
One Frog 4
Oomp-Bean-Soup 2
Over-and-Under Relay 8

Paper Bag Drama 10
Paper Bag Puppets 10
Paper Bag Relay 8
Party Poke 97-10
Pass the Scissors 7
Pen and Pencil Mixers 34-3
Penny Puzzle 8
Pillow Case Relay 8
Pinwheel 8
Poison 4
Progressive Games Party 5
Promenade Mixer 2

Question Proverbs 5

Rhythm 4
Rotten Egg 4
Run, Sheep, Run 9

Sardines 8
Shaking Hands 2
Shifty Lines 8
Shoe Scramble 8
Shopping Bag Relay 8
Shouting Names 2
Situation Drama 10
Slap Jack 3
Slide Right 3
Smellavision 1
Snowstorm 2
Song Scramble 30
Square Relay 4
Squat 2
Stand a Minute 22
Stick in the Hole 94
Stir the Mush 73
Stop Ball 91
Stride Ball 91
String Handcuffs 17
Swami 77
Swat 43

Teakettle 49
Team Relay 87
This Is My Nose 39
Three Deep 38
Trio Mixer 33
Tunnel Chase 27
Tunnel Relay 88
Turkish Numbers 74

Up Jenkins 51

Waltz Mixer 3
What's In The Bag? 15
Wheelbarrow Relay 87
Whoops, Tommy 73
Who's the Leader? 50
Wink 47
Word Mixer 34